The Significance of Territory

The Significance of

Territory

JEAN GOTTMANN

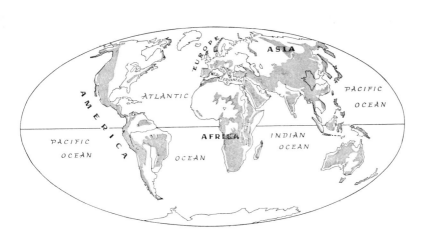

THE UNIVERSITY PRESS OF VIRGINIA
CHARLOTTESVILLE

Contents

Maps

Preface

WHEN the University of Virginia kindly invited me to deliver the Page-Barbour Lectures for 1971, giving me complete freedom to select my subject, I chose to speak on the concept of *territory*. I have been interested in this matter for some thirty years, during which I have seen the significance of territory for nations evolve in several ways. The attitude of people toward their territory has always been a basic relationship in geography, in politics, and in economics; in the fast-moving circumstances of our time this relationship was shifting and indeed needed reconsideration.

Amazingly little has been published about the concept of territory, although much speech, ink, and blood have been spilled over territorial disputes. To politicians, territory means the population and the resources therein, and sometimes also the point of honor of Irredentist claims. To the military, territory is topographic features conditioning tactical and strategic considerations as well as distance or space to be played with; occasionally it is also resources in terms of local supplies. To the jurist, territory is jurisdiction and delimitation; to the specialist in international law it is both an attribute and the spatial extent of sovereignty. To the geographer, it is the portion of space enclosed by boundary lines, the location and internal characteristics of which are to be described and explained.

To the specialist interested in political geography, and I happen to be one, territory appears as a material, spatial notion establishing essential links between politics, people, and the natural setting. Under a purely analytical approach, the notion of territory would break up and dissolve into a multitude of different concepts such as location, natural resources, population density, settlement patterns, modes of life, and so forth. The important aspect of territory as the unit in the political organization of space that defines, at least for a time, the relationships between the community and its habitat on one hand, and between the community and its neighbors on the other, has been little explored.

It seemed to me a timely and worthwhile subject to discuss. Territory turned out to be an elusive entity, as it is not the "body politic" which is people, but the support on which the body politic rests and without which it lacks balance and position in space. It is a shifting concept because it is an expression of political organization, which has operated through time according to changing principles. Some of the relations of a community with its habitat remain constant, and discussion of them may go back to Plato and earlier. But the momentum of recent history has modified a great deal of the environmental circumstances of politics, and it seemed useful for a better understanding of our time to reconsider the significance of territory and its evolution.

This is what I attempted to do in the three Page-Barbour Lectures of 1971; the text has been somewhat expanded in this book to allow for a fuller discussion of abundant and involved data. Too often territory has been examined mainly as an instrument for defense and supply, and its value assessed only in case of crisis. I have studied the significance of territory within the routine of the political process and within the framework of the development of civilization. I have limited my analysis mainly to "Western" concepts and history, leaving aside the territorial concepts in the Asiatic and African cultures of which I have little knowledge. My approach has followed historical logic. The concept of territory appears in this study as a psychosomatic device and its evolution as closely related to the human striving for security, opportunity, and happiness.

It has been an exciting and rewarding task. It seemed fitting to discuss these matters for the University of Virginia; at least three great Virginians, Thomas Jefferson, James Monroe, and Woodrow Wilson, among others, have substantially contributed in shaping our present concept of territory. I wish also to express my sincere appreciation to Professor Neill H. Alford, Jr., chairman of the Page-Barbour Lectures Committee, for all his understanding and helpfulness.

J. G.

Oxford
September 1971

The Significance of Territory

The People and Their Territory:
The Partitioning of the World

CIVILIZED people seem to have early aspired to universality, but they have always partitioned the space around them carefully to set themselves apart from their neighbors. At the earliest stages the area thus demarcated was meant to serve as the "home" of a primitive group—firstly, a shelter against aggression by outsiders, and secondly the feeding grounds, that is, the area wherefrom the resources for survival were to be obtained. One could probably equate such districting with the notion of territory, the first purpose of which is to fence off a portion of space for the security of its inhabitants.

To some extent the division of the land among primitive tribes can be compared to the partitioning of space among groups of animals. But the comparison cannot be carried very far, for civilized man would not live by security alone.[1] Discussing the origins of political organization, Aristotle described the formation of the Greek city-state, the *polis,* in a much-quoted passage of the *Politics:* "When several villages are united in a single complete community, large enough to be nearly or quite self-sufficing, the state comes into existence, originating in the bare needs of life, and continuing in existence for the sake of a good life" (1. 2. 1252b). Whatever the exact meaning of "a good life," it connotes a higher level of development of the locality—or shall we say, of the territory assigned to the state—than "the bare needs of life." Striving for the good life assumes improvement of the resources and living conditions of the

[1] Early geographers, such as Friedrich Ratzel, were impressed by the work of the botanists of the nineteenth century about the territorial extension and fluctuations of certain plants; they compared the rivalry between some states and empires with observations made in the botanical world. Today, an interesting, specialized literature is available, written by zoologists, on the territorial instincts or behavior of animal species. Some geographers have tried to transfer, somewhat hastily, conclusions about animals into the realm of political geography. (See Edward W. Soja, *The Political Organization of Space* [Washington, D.C., 1971].) However imperfect, our knowledge of the history, politics, and territorial requirements of people is much greater and better than our knowledge of the territorial behavior of animal species. An examination of the significance of territory to people can seldom gain by reference to the work of zoology.

place. To decide how to proceed and what the public good must be, a political organization has to be brought into existence, which in turn can function adequately only within a defined territorial framework small enough for the organization to control it.

The close association between the notion of political organization and the geographically defined concept of a territorial base begins very early in history, long before Aristotle. In the Old Testament, separate territory is presented as a necessary condition of freedom and independence as Moses takes the Hebrews out of Egypt to the Promised Land. As soon as the Promised Land is reached, the question of jurisdiction by a political structure over the people and the land arises, and the problems of diplomatic or military relations with neighbors appear at the same time. The Bible deals with these matters in the Book of Judges and the Books of Kings. The relationship of territory with jurisdiction and sovereignty over what happens in it, is an essential one. It clearly differentiates the people's territory from what may be described as territorial organization among certain animal species. To understand the past and present partitioning of the inhabited world, it is necessary to consider the unit in this partitioning, that is, to consider territory as a portion of space defined by a system of laws and a unity of government. Let us then turn to the lawyers' opinion in the matter.

Territory and Sovereignty

All the tenets of modern international law assign to territory an essential role in relations between national states. A state's territory outlines the geographical extent of its jurisdiction and its position in major aspects of external relations, such as proximity, contiguity, distance, and access to the sea. Professor Charles de Visscher wrote thus on the meaning of territory:

The firm configuration of its territory furnishes the State with the recognized setting for the exercise of its sovereign powers. The at least relative stability of this territory is a function of the exclusive authority that the State exercises in it and of the coexistence beyond its frontiers of political entities endowed with similar prerogatives.

This stability is above all a factor of security, of the security that peoples feel in the shelter of recognized frontiers—a confidence that has grown in them with the consolidation, in a community of aspirations and memories, of the bonds uniting them to the soil that they occupy. It is this sentiment that explains the extreme sensitiveness of opinion to everything that touches territorial integrity. . . . It is because the State is a territorial organization that violation of its frontiers is inseparable from the idea of aggression against the State itself.[2]

Agreeing with this statement and those of many other authorities, Professor R. Y. Jennings adds: "The mission and purpose of traditional international law has been the delimitation of the exercise of sovereign power on a territorial basis."[3] The practice of international law binds sovereignty and territory closely together. It would seem indeed that sovereignty needs territory on which it is to be exercised, and a territory would appear useless for all practical purposes unless it was under some recognized sovereignty.

Such is the legal position in the middle of the twentieth century, when practically all the land area of the planet has been surveyed and apportioned to some national or international authority to administer. State sovereignty has been extended to the air space above the land and to the bottom of the shallow seas according to a principle of contiguity to national territory. The great majority of the territorial units that have resulted from the political partitioning of the land have achieved political independence and may therefore exercise sovereignty within their borders. The links between territory and sovereignty are reinforced by the technological tools available to governments for the display of authority over vast geographical areas. Contemporary circumstances thus concur to bring out territorial sovereignty as a basic relationship of public law and international relations.

It has not always been so. The significance of territory has evolved considerably in the past and even during the twentieth century; this evolution was largely due to two powerful factors that have modified the very nature of sovereign power: firstly, technological progress freed people from their tight bonds to the nourishing soil and gradually increased the mobility of people and goods; secondly, sovereign power came to be increasingly vested in the mass of the people and exercised by elected representatives. Both

[2] Charles de Visscher, *Theory and Reality in Public International Law*, trans. P. E. Corbett (Princeton, N.J., 1957), pp. 197–98. The recent and monumental work by J. H. W. Verzijl, *International Law in Historical Perspective*, Vol. III: *State Territory* (Leyden, 1970), deals only briefly with the concept and nature of territory. Verzijl insists on the idea of "eminent domain" as the forerunner of territorial sovereignty. Despite its title this volume pays little attention to territory *per se* but offers a learned and useful summary of the procedures of acquisition and loss of territory and of the legal questions affecting sovereignty over the more debatable components of a state's territory, such as adjacent seas, inland lakes, international rivers, frontiers.

[3] R. Y. Jennings, *The Acquisition of Territory in International Law* (Manchester, 1963), p. 2.

trends curiously concurred in making people, whether as individuals or as groups, less dependent on the traditional structures for enforcing authority, and the basis for the enforcement of the law subtly shifted from allegiance to a personal sovereign toward controls exercised by the sovereign power in geographical space. The partitioning of space thus acquired an increasing significance, and territorial sovereignty became an essential expression of the law, coinciding with effective jurisdiction.[4]

However, it must never be forgotten that the relationship between sovereignty and territory is built upon a connecting link: *the people* in the territory or, if it is devoid of permanent settlement, at least *the activities of people* within the territory.

To maintain rights to a territory, the sovereign power must act in it continuously, or at least recurrently, and such action is carried out normally by human agents. Discussing the modes of acquisition of territory in modern times, Professor Jennings often refers to the arbitration decision by Judge Max Huber in the *Island of Palmas* case (1928). Judge Huber wrote that "the continuous and peaceful display of territorial sovereignty (peaceful in relation to other States) is as good as a title," and elaborated thus: "International law . . . cannot be presumed to reduce a right such as territorial sovereignty, with which almost all international relations are bound up, to the category of an abstract right, without concrete manifestations."[5]

Concrete manifestations of sovereignty are obvious and constant in a territory that is permanently inhabited and where laws are applied. The matter becomes more involved where human presence occurs seldom. The sovereign power is supposed to ascertain authority in such places by recurrent visits of its agents. The sole presence of a flag flying over the place may not be successful in maintaining sovereignty if activities are occasionally carried out there without the power's knowledge by people who do not recognize its authority. An international incident developed in 1945 between the United States and France when without prior consent from Paris the U.S. Navy landed a party of American seamen on the desert atoll of Clipperton, a tiny, recognized French territory in the Pacific, to carry out necessary observations in the war against Japan.

[4] Ian Brownlie, *Principles of Public International Law* (Oxford, 1966), gives in his analysis of territorial sovereignty (pp. 98–117) very relevant examples of this trend, and he states: "Ultimately, territory cannot be distinguished from jurisdiction for certain purposes" (p. 107).

[5] See Jennings, *Acquisition of Territory*, pp. 5 and 88–126, quoting from the official text of the decision.

To secure the French position, despite official American assurances that the temporary presence of the naval party was not intended to challenge French sovereignty, the French Navy sent a ship to Clipperton, and a French officer set foot on the small island, displaying sovereign rights in traditional fashion.

Such a display may lead to complex debate in the case of areas to which access is even more difficult, such as parts of a sea or even of the sea bed. In these cases, it would be the rights of passage or of use of some resource that would concretely matter, and these could be attained without actual human presence by means of a ship, a net, a cable, or a pipe. At present such installations are still operated from manned ships or platforms. In a time of increasing automation it is quite possible that human presence in the area would be entirely dispensed with, as all activities could be carried on by robots under remote control. When in 1959 the Soviet Union landed the first man-made missile on the moon, carrying among other items a copy of the Soviet national emblem, the question of whether the Soviets intended to claim sovereignty rights on that newly opened territory was immediately raised. The Soviet government denied any such intention, and later the United States indicated that the landings of American astronauts on the moon and the flying of the flag at the landing sites did not constitute any claim on surrounding territory. Although human activity required human presence in the past, it remains possible, in an era of developing automation, that the controllers of activities in portions of space claimed by certain powers will have to be recognized as exercising sovereignty over certain areas by indirect means.

As in all legal matters, territorial sovereignty is not separable from a definite human will and purpose. The concept of territory, though geographical, because it involves accessibility and therefore location, must not be classified with physical, inanimate phenomena. Although its Latin root, *terra,* means "land" or "earth," the word *territory* conveys the notion of an area around a place; it connotes an organization with an element of centrality, which ought to be the authority exercising sovereignty over the people occupying or using that place and the space around it. In its modern and legal use, it has come to designate a portion of geographical space under the jurisdiction of certain people. It signifies also a distinction, indeed a separation, from adjacent territories that are under different jurisdictions.

Law, politics, and jurisdiction are specific to humans, and more particularly, to civilized people. It was when organizing themselves, and the space they use, for the purposes of civilization that people found it necessary to partition in clear, systematic manner the spaces to which they had access. In that process the concept of territory was elaborated, with the forms and patterns that ensued.

The examination of the relations binding together territory and sovereignty have led us to begin to understand the meaning of territory. The two concepts are bound to evolve together, though not necessarily along the same track. We shall have the opportunity in the following chapters to deal at length with various aspects of the evolution from which the present situation issued. It may be important at this point to stress the considerable change developing in our time in the notion of sovereignty even in the view of competent lawyers, for such a change could not help but foster more evolution in the practical significance of territory. Indeed, some reports of American committees have hinted that, in view of the growing interdependence among the increasingly numerous independent states, no state could claim to be "sovereign" in the full old sense of the term.

In his individual opinion in the *Corfu Channel* case (Judgment of April 9, 1949) Judge Alvarez of the International Court of Justice stated:

By sovereignty we understand the whole body of rights and attributes which a State possesses in its territory, to the exclusion of all other States and also in relations with other States. Sovereignty confers rights upon States and imposes obligations on them.

These rights are not the same and are not exercised in the same way in every sphere of international law. I have in mind the four traditional spheres—terrestrial, maritime, fluvial and lacustrine—to which must be added three new ones—aerial, polar and floating (floating islands). The violation of these rights is not of equal gravity in all these different spheres.

Some jurists have proposed to abolish the notion of the sovereignty of States, considering it obsolete. That is an error. This notion has its foundation in national sentiment and in the psychology of the peoples, in fact it is very deeply rooted. The constituent instrument of the International Organization has especially recognized the sovereignty of States and has endeavoured to bring it into harmony with the objects of that Organization.

This notion has evolved, and we must now adopt a conception of it which will be in harmony with the new conditions of social life. We can no longer regard sovereignty as an absolute and individual right of every State, as used to be done under the old law founded on the individualist regime, according to which States were only bound by the rules which they had accepted. To-day, owing to social interdependence and to the predominance of the general interest, the States are bound by many rules which have not been ordered by their will. The sovereignty of the States has now become an *institution,* an *international social function* of a psychological character, which has to be exercised in accordance with the new international law.[6]

This statement, written in 1949, was well ahead of its time; it pointed out two important trends in the evolution of the concept of territory: the growing recognition of the psychological underpinning of territorial sovereignty, also acknowledged in the writings of Charles de Visscher, and the transformation of national sovereignty into an "international social function." It may be quite helpful for our understanding of the present meaning of "territory" to think of it as a geographical expression both of a social function and of an institution rooted in the psychology of peoples.

Moreover, Judge Alvarez, by enumerating the old and new "spheres" of international law, vividly illustrates the diversity of the geographical environment in which the law operates and sovereignty is exercised. As the plurality of spheres increases with the development of means of access to them, the variety of geographical features assumes greater importance in the consideration of territorial rights. That the gravity of the violation of such rights varies with the kind of "sphere" in which the violation has been perpetrated demonstrates the role of the geographical characteristics of territory in international matters, as well as in the internal administration of nations.

Political Aims in Organizing Space

People early and systematically partitioned the geographical space in which they lived. The concept of territory expresses the recognition of the fact that a group of people is at home in and has safe control of only a *fraction* of the total area that may be generally open to the wanderings and enterprises of its members. The concept connotes a certain reasonableness of human communities in their acceptance of geographical limitation for certain purposes, the foremost of which has been *security.*

Security must be organized against outsiders first, and within the community itself afterwards. Initially, it involves full control of all routes and means of access to an area. With a limited number of people, and before the extraordinary means provided by modern electronics and automation, access could be controlled more easily

[6] *International Court of Justice Reports* (The Hague, 1949), p. 43. Quoted in Edvard Hambro, *The Case Law of the International Court,* IIIA (Leyden, 1963), pp. 345–47.

if the area was not widespread. Extending the area would require increasing the number of people entrusted with the functions insuring security; these could form only a part of the total population and would have to be entirely trustworthy. To reinforce themselves most communities could not afford to bring into their midst outsiders whose subsistence was costly and whose loyalty would be constantly questioned; collective psychology combined with economics and demography to make it necessary in the past to outline territorial partitions. Old legends stress the role of geometric forms in the design of cities, palaces, and their walls: Dido, for instance, won the competition in Carthage by using the circle to trace the line of enclosure. The circle had a sacred character perhaps because the sun and the moon were round, but also because it was, as a few initiated people knew, the shortest circumference of a given area.

Thus the political partitioning of geographical space started and developed on a modest areal scale. Territory was the land belonging to and administered by a town; the word *territorium* seems to have been used with that meaning in medieval statutes in Florence, but the notion certainly existed in ancient Greece (where a *polis* had frontiers), in Phoenicia, and in Mesopotamia.[7] The narrow scope of the original territory of a people was good for physical security but discouraging to the quest for opportunity beyond the bare necessities of life, beyond the resources of the *status quo*.

The yearning for improvement and economic progress has not been the only psychological trait that has led men, even in prehistoric times, to wander beyond the safe horizon. One must take into account the urges, deeply rooted in human nature, for exploration and adventure, and for the possession of strange objects perhaps endowed with extraordinary properties. Strange objects must come from remote places. The earliest objects of trade found by archeologists seem to have been amulets: pieces of amber, crystals, curiously colored stones, and later brilliant pieces of metal. We have not yet given up our taste for gold and diamonds, or even amber and coral. For reasons metaphysical as well as basely materialistic, men endeavored to broaden the scope of their opportunity beyond the boundaries of their native territory, developing external relations for trade, war, and peace. The purposes of politics followed the movements of people: to the provision of security at home was

---

[7] Leo Oppenheim, *Ancient Mesopotamia* (Chicago, 1964), quotes (p. 121) concerning the *kidinnu* (freedom) status of Babylonian cities a letter sent by the inhabitants of Babylon to King Assurbanipal (seventh century B.C.) asserting that "even a dog is free when he enters the city of Babylon." The statement assumes a clear definition in the field of Babylon's territory.

added the securing of resources abroad. Domestic and foreign politics converged and interfered. Boundaries delimiting territory shifted. The partitioning of the geographical space became a constant, prime concern of the political process.

Human psychology was, of course, at the root of the matter; but people were to some extent conditioned by certain characteristics of the environment, especially by the basic facts that the world around them was *accessible*—for men would not have wandered around if they could not—and that it was endowed with a variety of physical forms that *diversified* the conditions of accessibility: land, sea, and air, the elements, climatic zones, mountain barriers, epidemics, and so forth. Even after sending expeditions to the moon, we are puzzled by the different conditions of accessibility to other planets as reported by the probes sent toward Mars and Venus. Regarding the earth itself one needs only to refer to the various spheres of territorial sovereignty, traditional and new, alluded to by Judge Alvarez in 1949.

Accessibility is, of course, the central and most permanent problem, as well as the indirect reason for the partitioning of space, regulating the conditions of access. A community fences a territory off to control the access of outsiders to its land, people, and resources. Still, the same community wants to enable its members to gain some access to the space, peoples, and resources of the outside world. Thus, within the common environment that geography studies and politics manipulates, defined as *the space accessible to human activities* (i.e. to people and the tools in their use and control) a constant conflict exists between the political purposes of greater security on the one hand and broader opportunity on the other.

Means of securing accessibility have shifted so fast in recent times that accessible space appears to have kept few stable characteristics. In fact, however, powerful political means for correcting the fluidity and restoring some stability have been created. At the time of the conquistadores it usually took six to eight weeks to cross the Atlantic; modern airliners fly across the same ocean in six to eight hours; but it may well take six weeks or more to obtain the official documents needed to make the trip. The skills of bureaucracy know how to compensate for the acceleration of transport. Circumstances of accessibility still vary from period to period and from country to country, even according to the allegiance of the individuals involved. Accessibility in space is organized, at all times in history, to serve political aims, and one of the major aims of politics is to regulate conditions of access.

However, geographical space, or the sum total of all territorial units (the whole space accessible to human activities) is endowed with a few constant and important features, which should now be outlined.

Characteristics of Accessible Space

As it is defined by its accessibility, geographical space must be, first of all, *continuous,* allowing access from one point within it to another. This continuity must exist not only in nature, but also, more importantly, in recognized knowledge. Before the Europeans discovered America, the lands that were to become a "New World" were not present in the continuous world then stretching from Iceland to China; they were not perceived as part of the geographical space of the "Old World" peoples. Similarly, Australia entered that space only after it was discovered, despite the mythical design appearing on many earlier maps, long before Captain Cook, of a *Terra Australis Incognita* in the southern seas. Access requires, therefore, prior recognition of a spatial continuity. A place becomes potentially accessible, once known, owing to its physical continuity with known territory. If the continuity is interrupted, either by lack of knowledge or by a physical barrier, a limit is drawn to the system defined as geographical space.

While continuous, geographical space is *limited.* The limits have varied and will vary; they must be described as of a specific date. The limits of their geographical space were not at all the same for the inhabitants of the island we call Manhattan in A.D. 1200, in 1900, and in 1971. In the year 1200, the world accessible to the Indians who lived in Manhattan was completely different from and much narrower than the world accessible to the inhabitants of the islands of Great Britain and Corsica. How similar may have been the worlds of the English and Corsicans in that year could be the subject of an interesting discussion; geographical knowledge was at that time the privilege of a few; but the two European areas, though insular and somewhat isolated, maintained various communications; both had been raided by the Norse and had sent men to the Crusades. In 1900 the world accessible to the people in all three islands was the same in terms of its limits. It was again the same for the people in those three areas in terms of common limits of potential accessibility in 1971; but the potential had greatly expanded from 1900 to 1971, to include the moon and vast areas of interplanetary space which, though known and observed with telescopes in and before 1900, were considered inaccessible to people. Besides physical continuity and recognized knowledge, technology greatly contributes, of course, to the determination of the limits of accessibility.

Though limited, and in many respects finite, geographical space is *expanding*. It has been expanding for a long time, in irregular but continuous fashion. The impulse of exploring beyond the recognized, safe horizon of the moment has always been bothering the human mind. To foster exploration the necessary tools for transport and observation are devised, then improved, to make steadily more and more accessible each area added to the frontiers of geographical space. An extraordinary sprawl of the geographical knowledge beyond long established limits was started with the discoveries of the great navigators in the fifteenth century: the Portuguese rounded Africa, and Columbus and the Spanish expeditions that followed brought the Americas into the Europeans' accessible space. Detailed exploration of the newly opened maritime and continental spaces has proceeded since at a steady pace. As men reached the North and South Poles, surveyed the hearts of the great deserts, and scaled the highest mountains, our world seemed to take on a complete, finite, spatial shape. But the scientific and technical advances of the twentieth century gave a new impulse and great acceleration to the expansion of accessibility in several other directions.

Twenty years ago, I wrote to show how the world's political partitioning results from the degree of accessibility:

> The sovereignty of the moon has no importance whatsoever to-day because men cannot reach it nor obtain anything from it. The Antarctic had no political standing before navigators began going there, but since it was made accessible by its discoverers, the icy continent has been divided into portions like an apple pie—and all these portions are distinct political compartments in which a number of international incidents have occurred. When the first explorers land on the moon, the earth's satellite will pass from the field of astronomy to the geography textbooks, and lunar political problems will appear and grow steadily.[8]

As these lines are being written the space ship of the American Apollo XV expedition streaks back toward the earth, carrying with the three astronauts a cargo of geological samples from the moon. Permanent bases now function in Antarctica, maintained by several nations. Because the uses of the moon and of the Antarctic continent are still very limited, the political problems involved in jurisdictional disputes have been negligible in those areas. But where active use of substantial resources is involved as is already the case

[8] Jean Gottmann, "The Political Partitioning of Our World: An Attempt at Analysis," *World Politics*, IV (July 1952), p. 513.

for the geological strata under the continental shelf, jurisdiction has been attributed to riparian powers, and territorial sovereignty has been extended to the newly accessible space.

The expansion of accessibility constantly increases the *diversity* of geographical space. Much of it is purely physical; there are obvious distinctions to be made, such as land, sea, air, and now also interplanetary space, as well as the depths under the ground and under the sea. Topography, climate, and vegetation add to the variety of local and regional conditions, and human action, past and present, multiplies the diversification. Political partitioning, while it lasts, strengthens differences existing on the two sides of each partition in terms of concrete structures, systems of vested interests, and psychological attitudes.

However, nature and man have long collaborated not only to partition and diversify geographical space but also to organize it. *Organization* assumes a purpose and a method. It involves a rationalization of the facts of diversity and complementarity observed in the various parts, or territories, of a partitioned world. Organization of space integrates the natural factors that govern the forces and the forms observed in physical space, and also integrates the many social, economic, and political forces that, manipulating the available technological lore, use the natural environment for the people's purposes.

This organization of space has been studied on the whole more systematically by geographers than any other learned profession; almost every scientific discipline, however, concerns itself with some particular aspect of the natural or the social environment, and has contributed to the common exploration of the whole system. It seems today that we have come to understand the purposes of human action better, or at least to describe them better, than the longer-range purposes of nature, which used to be confused a few centuries ago with the inscrutable purposes of Providence. We now know that the organization of space is largely determined by partitioning, which is inherent in physical diversity, but which is also politically molded, and often modified in its many local details, to fit the aim of providing the various communities in the space with as much security as seems possible.

Each compartment designed by the network of political partitions remains, however, interdependent with others located around it or more distant; this has been so because men seek the adventure of exploring beyond the immediate horizon, because the yearning for opportunity induces them to take advantage of their steadily improving mobility, and because sentimental and economic relation-

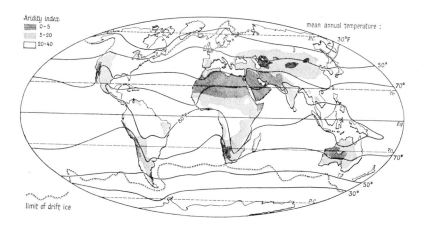

1 The Physical Variety of the Globe. Topographic (*above*) and climatic (*below*). The lines on the lower map indicate mean annual temperatures and the shading the degree of aridity of the climate.

ships have built into the whole structure more complementarity between the territorial units and between the communities, reducing
self-sufficiency in a narrow territorial frame to a last resort.

The Functions of Territory

To sum up, the space accessible to human activities may be described as continuous but partitioned, limited though expanding,
diversified and organized. The reasons for accessibility and organization, both willed by man and largely controlled by him, are
rooted in the desire to provide as much opportunity as possible—to
pursue "the good life." However, organization also intends to regulate access and opportunity, avoiding the threat of situations that
may be contrary to the accepted interests of the community. In this
respect it concurs with partitioning in an over-riding concern for
security.

If a territory is the model compartment of space resulting from
partitioning, diversification, and organization, it may be described
as endowed with two main functions: to serve on the one hand as
a shelter for security and on the other hand as a springboard for
opportunity. Both security and opportunity require an internal organization of the territory as well as a subsequent organization of
its external relations. An element of conflict is built into the functions of the territory, and behind them looms a contradiction in the
purposes of territorial sovereignty and of political independence:
the search for security will often clash with the yearning for broader
opportunity. The former calls for relative isolation, the latter for
some degree of interdependence with the outside.

However, the question arises of satisfying the people in the territory, for the sake of whom ultimately the territory has been
brought into existence. Would they be content with the kind and
amount of opportunity they might obtain within a very secure
framework? No durable security can be assured for a dissatisfied and
divided people, either in their domestic affairs or in their relations
with the outside. Professor Georges Scelle once wrote that the state,
as a political entity, is traditionally constituted of three bodily
components *(elements corporels)*, the population, the territory,
and the governmental organization, but that the territory could not
be considered simply a corporeal, concrete element of the body
politic. Rather, "the concern for the preservation of habitat exists
as a passionate psychological reflex in all human communities."[9]

[9] "L'Etat," in *Introduction à l'etude du droit* (Paris, 1951), I, pt. 1, 73–89
(quote p. 87) .

Whichever approach we attempt we seem to find the same confusing diagnosis: territory, although a very substantial, material, measurable, and concrete entity, is the product and indeed the expression of the psychological features of human groups. It is indeed a *psychosomatic* phenomenon of the community, and as such is replete with inner conflicts and apparent contradictions. Territorial sovereignty is an indispensable attribute of independent nations; the territory is the very basis on which national existence rests, the "sacred soil" in whose defense true citizens will be prepared to give their lives. The concept is one of self-preservation, but also one of preserving the community's way of life, the right to self-government, freedom, and whatever opportunity a free people is entitled to. If territory must coincide and coexist with a certain unity of jurisdiction, it is impregnated with the purposes of that legal function. The concept leads to a geography of ethics. To analyze territory better, it becomes necessary to examine its evolution in time and space.

II

Security versus Opportunity:
The Road to National Sovereignty

THE etymology of the word *territory*, if investigated in a host of dictionaries, turns out to be a rather moot question. In the western European languages the word comes certainly from the Latin *territorium*, and its systematic use is recorded from the late Middle Ages in English, French, and German texts. Examples abound from the fifteenth century on,[1] though much more ancient instances have been found, for example in Cicero.[2] The concept certainly existed and was debated in the earliest known works on politics, particularly by Plato.[3] The word was formed by adding to *terra* ("earth" or "land" in Latin) the suffix *torium*, which seems to have meant "belonging to" or "surrounding." Perhaps one may venture for *torium* the hypothesis of the root *tor*, from which derived *tower* and *tour*, and which conveyed in Medieval English and in Old French the meaning of both "a well-rounded building" and "a position of strength."

It is, therefore, quite logical that the first meaning indicated by the *Oxford English Dictionary* for *territory* would be "the land or district lying round a city or town and under its jurisdiction"; this definition, however, is listed as "obsolete" and followed by a second, more generally accepted and modern meaning: "the land or country belonging to or under the dominion of a ruler or state." Examples given for this second usage date back to 1494. One could infer that nowadays the national organization of the land has supplanted what used to be recognized as the prerogative of cities. Indeed, the early discussion of territorial questions related to Greek city-states, to Roman cities (certainly not to the Roman Empire, which had pretentions to universality), then to the medieval Italian cities, such as Florence, Pisa, Genoa, Milan, and Venice.

This reflects once more the evolution of the notion of sovereignty, to which territory is so intimately linked: city-states in ancient times, and in some regions during the Middle Ages, had territorial

---

[1] Especially as shown in the *Oxford English Dictionary*.
[2] Du Cange, *Glossarium mediae et infirmae latinitatis*.
[3] See below, pp. 17–20.

sovereignty, while the sovereignty of kings and princes rested on the allegiance of individuals or organized bodies, rather than on the possession of land areas. The essence of sovereignty was gradually transferred to the control of well-defined territory, and in that process the late fifteenth century was an important moment. The sixteenth century, however, was the decisive time in European affairs, when politics and legal doctrine began claiming territorial sovereignty as a prime attribute of kingdoms or states. By the end of the eighteenth century the notion of national sovereignty over well-delimited territory had come to the fore in political practice as well as in the theory of jurisprudence. What was started a very long time ago by ancient city-states, accelerated by the great geographical discoveries and the Reformation, came to fruition with the American and French revolutions.

The process was not, however, one of simple enclosure of the land by individual political communities or of sheer land-grabbing by certain princes or republics. It was accompanied by complex soul-searching by statesmen and philosophers as to where the public good was to be found, and where the best interest of their respective peoples lay. It reflected a moral debate as well as a practical need to organize for prosperity, war, and peace.

Plato's Search for Stability

The oldest analysis of the political significance of territorial characteristics is found in Plato's *Laws,* where the dialogue outlines how a new city-state ought to be planned. In the *Republic* Plato discussed his ideal of the *polis* from the moral and constitutional points of view; the approach in the *Laws* is much more geographical and sets the problems of the size, location, and use of territory in terms that have never lost their validity.

The first question to arise is where to locate the new city, which is to be planned, of course, on an island (4. 704–10). The *polis* itself and most of the population were to be settled inland, away from the seashore, to avoid insofar as possible contact with the sea and with maritime and overseas influences. All indispensable relations with the outside world would be dealt with by a small number of specialized civil servants. What should be the size of the territory of such an ideal *polis?* "The territory should be large enough for the maintenance of a certain number of men of modest ambition and no larger. The population should be sufficient to defend themselves against wrongs from societies on their borders, and to assist their neighbours when wronged to some purpose" (5. 737).

These two sentences are extremely suggestive. They sum up quite well the long debates that have unfolded about territorial disputes and the very concept of territorial *needs* during the twenty-four centuries that followed. The territory must be "large enough to maintain" but "no larger." Maintain according to what standards? Modest standards certainly, as the population is described: "a certain number of men of *modest ambition*." This is indeed the crux of the matter: Plato believes that a city-state ought to be as self-sufficient as possible, and he eliminates as far as possible the maritime and foreign trade from the potential economic resources, for he wants the society to be virtuous and peaceful, so that it can enjoy stable good government. Such government would not be possible if ambitious people, looking for more opportunity, engaged in maritime activities on a large scale, bringing the influences of foreign policy and foreign interests into daily domestic affairs. Every thinker, even Plato, must be read in the historical context of his time and country. Plato was worried about the politics of Athens; he attributed the evil elements in it largely to the influence of seamen and traders who from the Piraeus constantly intervened in Athenian political life. Athens had lost to Sparta in the Peloponnesian Wars; and Sparta was a rural, inland power, less mercantile, less rich, and more disciplined.

The *Laws,* as well as the *Republic,* is obviously influenced by Plato's admiration for Sparta, and by the general Spartan pattern of geographical and social organization. Too much of a theoretician to adhere just to one contemporary model, however, Plato based his reasoning on general moral considerations. "The fact is," says the Athenian, "the object we are keeping in view in our present investigations into topography and legislation is the moral worth of a social system; we do not agree with the multitude that the most precious thing in life is bare preservation in existence; we hold, as I think we have said before, that it is better to become thoroughly good and to remain so as long as existence lasts" (*Laws,* 4. 707).

Thus his precepts are not aimed at security only, but at virtue and happiness through "goodness." To achieve this goal, however, Plato insists that opportunity be strictly limited, firstly by screening the lure of overseas adventure, speculation, and profit, then secondly by restricting the extent of territory. In ancient times, and indeed until the Industrial Revolution that began in western Europe in the eighteenth century, there could have been only two major sources of wealth: income from the land, and profits from trade.

Sparta had based her economy on the produce of the land, Athens on maritime trade and business.

Plato is aware of the strict limitations on the resources a stable community may obtain from a small, stabilized territory. The technology of agricultural production changed little and seldom in those days, and Plato assumes its stability. To make sure that his ideal *polis,* having reached a certain moral state of goodness, does not lose it, he wants to protect the stability and continuity of the economic base and of the political structure. Hence two conditions: the first is qualitative, as the people must be of "modest ambition"; the second is quantitative, as the population should be "sufficient to defend themselves against wrongs" but not allowed to increase much.

If the population increased, the balance between needs and resources in the limited territory would be upset, and a political change might lead to diverse moves toward the broadening of the scope of opportunity. For such situations, Plato's answer is either population control to avoid an increase in numbers or the emigration of the surplus population to a new place, which ought to be settled according to the same pattern, the population being kept away from the seashore. The ideal settlement and political organization suggested in the *Laws* assumes firstly an unlimited supply of empty islands to be settled, and secondly a people so content with its condition and so aware of its goodness and happiness that no change would be attempted.

Like any system of laws, Plato's aims at achieving moral standards and the happiness that comes as their reward. Although security, as he insists, is not the only purpose, it is an essential component of the happiness and stability he seeks. Opportunity is strictly rationed in order to avoid stirring up ambitions that could develop into greed.

The Platonic scheme of partitioning geographical space has had a lasting impact on political and social thought. Its compartments would be inward-looking quadrangles with a somewhat monastic character, and more like those of a Chartreuse than those of the expansionist abbeys of the Order of Cluny or of the Templar Knights. The utopians and socialists of the nineteenth century offered designs of similar partitioning from Fourier's *phalanstère* to Ebenezer Howard's "garden cities."

Perhaps no better illustration can be found of this kind of philosophy in practice than the policies of Japan during the period of the Tokugawa isolation (mid-seventeenth to mid-nineteenth centuries). Japan locked herself in her archipelago, forbade entrance to foreigners, and reduced external relations to a trickle maintained through the small trading posts allowed to the Dutch and the Chinese in the harbor of Nagasaki. For two hundred years Japan led a secluded life almost *in vitro,* controlling its population to avoid the pressures of demographic growth. In the 1850s outside intervention opened up Japan and set it on a new course, catching up with the times, endeavoring to take the largest possible share of a suddenly expanded opportunity. This course led Japan into World War II and to bitter defeat.

In the shifts of a national policy from seclusion along a Platonic pattern to an ambitious exploitation of maximum opportunity, few examples in history are as spectacular as the story of Japan in recent centuries. Its lessons, however, are not convincing. Were the Japanese people happier in the period of the Tokugawa isolation than during the Meiji era of modernization and expansion? Or were they happier in the years following 1950 when, after the hardest time of reconstruction, the nation set out on a policy of rapid economic development and commercial expansion, though giving up military power under the American umbrella? No definitive answer can be given to this sort of question. The Japanese story only demonstrates that stability and isolation do not guarantee security for an indefinite period. Altogether Japan was probably quite lucky to have enjoyed successfully two centuries of deliberate seclusion. After 1850 the globe was approaching an organization into a complete, finite system of interconnected parts. The North Atlantic powers were fast expanding the network of their respective commercial and naval domains. The marginal position of Japan provided no adequate defense against the intervention of a stronger foreign power, armed with the overwhelming weapons of a much more advanced technology.

By examining the case in history which seems to have best illustrated territorial policies shaped along a philosophy similar to that argued in Plato's *Laws,* one is led to doubt that any simple rule can provide a guarantee of security. Cutting off a territory and the community inhabiting it from the mainstream of the world does not save it from external interference in the long run. The compartments of the partitioned system remain interdependent. Change in other compartments that participate more actively in the mainstream of evolution is bound to proceed faster than in the secluded part. The balance established when the seclusion began will not last indefinitely. Internal stability does not necessarily provide a community with the means for defense against the threats caused by the expansion of other powers.

Aristotle and the Lure of Opportunity

While its logic recurs constantly in a certain thread of political thought, the Platonic doctrine did not command much respect in ancient Greece. In fact Plato's own best pupil, Aristotle, started a very different trend. In his *Politics* (especially in Book II) he discusses at length Plato's ideas and the *Laws* in particular but without paying much attention to the territorial question. Aristotle is more interested in the constitutional and social organization of the state. In Book VII he comes to the relationship of people with territory:

> First among the materials required by the statesman is population: he will consider what should be the number and character of the citizens, and then what should be the size and character of the country. Most persons think that a state in order to be happy ought to be large; but even if they are right, they have no idea what is a large and what a small state. For they judge of the size of the city by the number of the inhabitants, whereas they ought to regard not their number, but their power. . . . Clearly, then, the best limit to the population of a state is the largest number which suffices for the purposes of life, and can be taken in at a single view.
>
> Much the same principle will apply to the territory of the state: everyone would agree in praising the territory which is most entirely self-sufficing, and that must be the territory which is all-producing, for to have all things and to want nothing is sufficiency. In size and extent it should be such as may enable the inhabitants to live at once temperately and liberally in the enjoyment of leisure. [7. 1326a–b]

Aristotle's principles seem to agree with Plato's on the desirability of self-sufficiency and on a rather limited size, but they differ greatly on the ways in which self-sufficiency and safety are attained. The reference to the "enjoyment of leisure" is an elaboration of the "good life" which is at obvious variance with the "modest ambition" of the more puritanical Plato. Aristotle proceeds to describe the general characteristics of the territory, which he wishes "difficult of access to the enemy and easy of egress to the inhabitants," an ideal that may be rather difficult to achieve in geography. He also wants the position of the city itself "well situated in regard both to sea and land," and in a conveniently central location. Then he elaborates the question of the relation to the sea and here clearly takes issue with Plato:

> Whether a communication with the sea is beneficial to a well-ordered state or not is a question which has often been asked. It is argued that

the introduction of strangers brought up under other laws, and the increase of population, will be adverse to good order; the increase arises
from their using the sea and having a crowd of merchants coming and
going, and is inimical to good government. Apart from these considerations, it would be undoubtedly better both with a view to safety and to
the provision of necessaries, that the city and territory should be connected with the sea . . . it is necessary that they should import from
abroad what is not found in their own country and that they should ex-
port what they have in excess; for a city ought to be a market, not indeed for others, but for herself. [7. 1327a]

Elaborating on the market function, Aristotle comes to suggest
that, though large-scale trade could make the place "a market for
the world," a state may limit any harm that this function may en-
tail by establishing the emporium outside city walls and enacting
laws to preserve the desired networks of communication and forms
of government. He even believes that a "moderate naval force . . .
commensurate with the scale of her enterprises" is advantageous to
a city (7. 1327b).

Book VII of the *Politics* is indeed an essential document in the
history of political thought. Here Aristotle lays the ground for the
trilogy of elements constituting a state: the population, the territory, and the unity of the system of government. That trilogy is still
quoted in most basic texts on the state in law and politics. In describing what characteristics the state should have for good order
and government, Aristotle opens the debate with Plato, stresses the
relationship between people and territory as well as the need to coordinate security with opportunity. He does not stress the conflict of
these as Plato did and as much ensuing political philosophy would
do.

It is interesting to the geographer and to the planner to observe
the importance assigned in the debate to the city's relation to the
sea and to the meaning of the centrality of the city in the state. Because he wants more resources, more opportunity for the enjoyment
of life, Aristotle approves the use of the major conveniences that
may be available. Sea navigation and maritime commerce are not
to be neglected; in fact, they are to be fully used by the Aristotelian
state, whose self-sufficiency is achieved through foreign trade as well
as local production. The state organizes its territory to be a regular
and full participant in the international system and does not seek
seclusion or isolation from it.

Regarding the organization of space, Aristotle's doctrine is more
in agreement with the traditional Greek view than Plato's. Many
city-states developed in locations that were inhospitable and had

very limited local resources. Their inhabitants had to earn their living by their wits, for their land did not yield enough products. A very remarkable case in this category was Delos, a powerful center that rose on a small and desolate island in the middle of the Aegean Sea. The Homeric hymn to Delian Apollo tells the story quite well: Leto, wife of Zeus, searched for a place on earth to give birth to Apollo:

So far roamed Leto in travail with the god who shoots afar, to see if any land would be willing to make a dwelling for her son. But they greatly trembled and feared, and none, not even the richest of them dared receive Phoebus, until queenly Leto set foot on Delos. . . .[4]

There a difficult negotiation ensued. Leto pointed out that by providing a sanctuary for Apollo they will make themselves safe and rich, although they "will never be rich in oxen and sheep, nor bear vintage nor yet produce plants abundantly . . . for truly your own soil is not rich." Delos knew it was small and poor; the Delians rejoiced at Leto's proposal but consented only after she swore that Apollo would not scorn them or do them any harm. Apollo was born in Delos; the island then blossomed with golden flowers and became a great meeting place for men "with swift ships and great wealth."

Delos was in Hellenistic and Roman times one of the major markets and maritime centers of the eastern Mediterranean. The location on such a small and rugged island of a powerful city and seaport was surprising. It still appears today as a marvel to the visitor who looks at the island bristling with the monumental remnants of great buildings, temples, villas, warehouses, and hostels—a sort of small Hellenistic Manhattan. Such unlikely development of the small territory was made possible first by the sanctuary function, which made it safe and an active center of pilgrimage, and later by a clever policy of alliances, shifting from the Ionian League to Athens, to Samos, and again to Athens, then to Egypt, and finally to Rome. In the first century B.C., involved in the maritime struggle between Rome and Athens, Delos was devastated and soon lost both its emporium and sanctuary functions. The island was abandoned after the second century A.D. Its story is perhaps the most remarkable example of a tiny and ill-shaped territory blooming with extraordinary prosperity for hundreds of years, to become only a monument to its own past.[5]

[4] *The Homeric Hymns*, 3, "To Delian Apollo," ll. 45–50. Trans. H. G. Evelyn-White, London, 1914.
[5] See P. Roussel, *Delos* (Paris, 1925) .

While the case of such a small and isolated island is surprising and striking, instances abound in the past and the present of rather small territories developing economic prosperity and political influence on a scale quite incommensurate with their area, population, or natural resources. Switzerland and the Netherlands are certainly examples among modern nations. In the ancient past city-states like Jerusalem, Athens, Rome, and later Venice started from awkward and narrow beginnings to build up wide empires. In a way the westward march across the American continent from small Atlantic bases may be related, to the same category of evolution. Once a community accepts it, the lure of opportunity often leads to rapid territorial expansion.

The Appeal of Universality

Aristotle himself provides the first example in Western political philosophy of the trend of thought that leads from the definition of the characteristics of a limited, modest state, existing among many others, to a plan of great universal imperium.

In Book VII of the *Politics*, he proceeds to discuss the character of the citizens of various states. He describes the Europeans, "full of spirit but wanting in intelligence and skill . . . and incapable of ruling others"; then the Asians, who accept subjection and slavery because, though "intelligent and inventive, [they are] wanting in spirit." Now he comes to the Greeks: "But the Hellenic race, which is situated between them, is likewise intermediate in character, being high-spirited and also intelligent. Hence it continues free, and is the best-governed of any nation, and if it could be formed into one state, would be able to rule the world" (7. 1327b).

The power of the king of Macedonia was beginning to cast its shadow over the whole of Greece. Aristotle was tutoring the young prince Alexander. "If it could be formed into one state"—the dream of Hellenistic unity foreshadowing the Greek supremacy over Asia as well as Europe. This famous passage of *Politics* testifies to the early, mystical idea of the central geographical position determining political supremacy, and it also indicates the sort of ideas of universal domination Aristotle may well have taught to his royal pupil.

Alexander put his education into practice. He learned fast; soon after his conquest of Persia he understood the need for some decentralization and for admitting the peoples in the conquered territories to partnership in the administration of his rapidly expanding empire. The Greeks, and Aristotle himself, did not agree easily to such broad and generous views of the rights to be conceded to people they considered barbarians, beginning with the Persians.

Alexander was, of course, pursuing a policy of Hellenization of the world, though an enlightened one. He appears to have linked his concept of the Hellenistic way of life with urbanization and with a steady flow of commercial relations binding together the lands of the empire. Such views were certainly opposed to the Platonic principles but may well have been derived from Aristotle's teaching. They were also probably the fruit of careful observation of the Greek area over which the Macedonians extended their supremacy. The Middle East still bears the imprint of Alexander's planning and establishment of new cities. Many were called Alexandria. The most important of them, a great commercial and cultural metropolis for many centuries, Alexandria of Egypt, was set in the delta of the Nile; another Alexandria, of which Karachi is the modern successor, was planted in the delta of the Indus. Alexander planned a network of seaport cities, located near the mouths of great rivers, as major commercial hinges and hubs of his empire. Territorial expansion proceeded along a master plan of spatial organization such as had probably never been seen before. This great design must have been one of the reasons for the young conqueror's immense and lasting popularity.

There was really no territorial limit assigned to the expansion on which Alexander launched, leading the united Greeks and Macedonians. The imperial concept, possibly based on Book VII of the *Politics*, had a universal character. Perhaps this stage in ancient history has to be viewed from a different angle than the too narrow relationship of a young prince and his tutor: the Greek city-state had matured in the fourth century B.C. to a point where it could be fully examined, analyzed, and debated by philosophers, and this analysis reaches a sort of perfection with Aristotle's writings.[6] Alexander's reign came after the city-state had had its heyday. Many of the cities had grown to a size that required more systematic political coordination, and they depended on an intricate system of interrelationships.

This evolution had also penetrated the kingdoms of larger territorial extent in Egypt and in the southwest Asia. The quasi-miraculous speed and success of Alexander, in a short time and over such a vast area, could be more easily understood if these events brought to fruition a well-advanced trend toward interconnectedness in the Hellenistic world and in the countries that the Greeks

[6] The *Politics* is the essential but not the only work of Aristotle in this respect. His *Constitution of Athens* belongs in the same line.

called "barbarian." The network of relations of a center such as Delos from the fifth to the second centuries B.C. would confirm such a trend. And with the suddenly and immensely expanded political framework achieved by Alexander, the idea of the universality of empire spread in the ancient world.

Alexander the Great died young in 323 B.C., his work certainly unfinished according to his own plans. It has been observed that Demosthenes, the great defender and advocate of the independence of the city-states, committed suicide the following year. True, Alexander's generals broke up the unity of the empire and divided it into several realms where different dynasties arose, making war on one another. However, kingdoms with much wider territories than those of the Greek city-states resulted from these divisions; a common Hellenistic culture and economic system endured, linking the various kingdoms together and preparing for the Roman take-over, which was completed in less than three centuries all around the Mediterranean, to the Danube, the Rhine, and the Tyne.

With Roman supremacy, the imperium took on a definitely universal quality in doctrine and even in practice. Even the wars with the barbarians along the limes were considered almost as civil disturbances along a steadily advancing frontier. The empire stopped at the physical barriers of the great deserts, the oceans, and the Hercynian forests of Europe. Beyond these barriers Rome knew, of course, of the existence of other distant empires. Some commercial relations were maintained with India and China, and with the less organized and even more barbaric areas of northern Europe and of Africa south of the Sahara. Accessibility to these remote parts was, however, so difficult and irregular that it hardly affected the doctrine of the universality of Rome's domination.

Within the regularly accessible space, Rome applied a policy of systematic planning, homogenizing the system of laws and the ways of life, and developing increasing economic interdependence. Her imperial network of communications by sea and land still amazes us; the Roman roads still underscore the present system of highways in many countries from England to the Sinai. The territorial concept was, however, in use within the empire, but applied to what was the equivalent of local government: the Latin meaning of *territorium* referred to districts around the cities that were the pillars of the imperial political structure.

Indeed the Roman system and administrative doctrine may best be expressed by the formula *urbi et orbi*. When in the fourth century A.D. the location of the supreme power of the Caesars in the city, the old Rome, did not appear to fit the current needs of universality as well as it had in the past, the emperor Constantine could make the decision of moving his headquarters to a new Rome, on the Bosporus. Sir John Myres has aptly analyzed the strategic elements involved in the choice of Constantinople:

> If the New Rome was to defend the empire as a whole, it must be as near as possible, not only to the Danube frontier and to the northwestern trunk-road, by which Aquileia and Milan were to give and receive reinforcements, but to the Euphrates frontier as well. If it was to be a great centre of population, it must be fed; so it must stand on the seaboard within reach of the corn of Egypt, as well as any which might still come from the steppe ports. . . . In case of accidents to resources from overseas, it must have local supplies, and a local reserve of men; so it must command the Thracian cornlands and highlands as Lysimachia and Adrianople had done but without the risk of isolation which hampered both of these. . . . It must be essentially Greek for it was to dominate the sentiments as well as the interests of the Greeks.[7]

The Caesars could plan a network of several Romes just as Alexander the Great visualized a network of Alexandrias. The concept of universal empire had uprooted the seat of power. But Constantine did not present the decision of transfer as an act of sheer imperial policy; he announced that it was dictated by divine will as seen by the emperor in a vision.[8] Rome and Constantinople were good capitals not so much because they were great crossroads as because they were *mystical* crossroads.

Constantine was the first Caesar to become a Christian. A religion with a universal doctrine was spreading through the Roman world. The political structure of the world was gradually taking on a religious, metaphysical connotation. For a millenium the significance of territory in Europe was to be reduced to very little indeed, even on the local scale.

Individual Allegiance versus Territory

The pressure of the Barbarians advancing on the marches of the empire was beginning to overwhelm the imperial structure. A definite partition into Eastern and Western Empires, under two emperors, was agreed upon in A.D. 395, but a few years later the Visigoths invaded Italy, and in 410 their king, Alaric, sacked Rome.

[7] Sir John Myres, "The Marmara Region," in *Geographical History in Greek Lands* (Oxford, 1953), p. 240.

[8] See A. Alföldi, *The Conversion of Constantine and Pagan Rome* (Oxford, 1948), and Ferdinand Lot, *La fin du monde antique* (Paris, 1927).

The Eastern Emperor in Byzantium could still claim some universal competence in his functions, but the *Codex Theodosianus* in 438 legally separated the eastern and western sections of the empire. In the west the territorial extent of the emperor's authority shrank rapidly. The supreme authority in Rome was shared, in fact, by the emperor with the bishop of Rome. In 452 it was Pope Leo I who actually stopped the Huns of Attila advancing in Italy, but he could not prevent the sack of Rome by the Vandals in 455.

Imperial authority lost its territorial base in the west, and became nomadic in practice. The solution appeared now in using the cultural superiority of the Roman system and the moral superiority of the Christian faith, well established in Rome by that time, to convert the Germanic and Slavonic tribes to Christianity and re-establish a unified order based on the faith. The individual and tribal allegiance to a sovereign and to the Church became the essential framework of social and political structure. Indeed, European society in the period from the fifth to the twelfth centuries was too fluid and nomadic to give any substance to a territorial concept.

At times, however, the need for some demarcation arose, and the drawing of a few boundaries on the map hints at the persistence of the concept, somewhere in the background of the political process. Geographic knowledge had declined since Ptolemy and Strabo, and maps were often inaccurate. Individuals drew their rights from the group they belonged to rather than the place they came from. As the Middle Ages unfolded, three events caused geographical partitioning with lasting territorial and cultural consequences.

In the seventh century the prophet Mohammed preached a new faith in Arabia, starting in the Middle East the fundamental cleavage between Islam and Christianity. With a powerful impulse to universality, the Arabs started soon after the Hegira (622) an extraordinarily sweeping expansion, taking Damascus in 635, Jerusalem in 638, conquering Egypt by 642, Persia in 643, the Punjab by 664 and North Africa from 670 to 680. Several times they thrust toward Constantinople, laying siege to the imperial city for the first time in 669. Early in the eighth century they were established in Spain, where the caliphate of Cordoba was founded in 755.

A first great "iron curtain" descended then between the realms dominated by the two different faiths: Christianity and Islam. The curtain cut across the Mediterranean, isolating Europe from the lands in Asia and Africa that had been colonized by the Hellenistic and Roman empires. Two fronts were established: one across Anatolia in the east, threatening Constantinople, the other dividing Spain in the west, with frequent incursions into southwestern

France. Naval warfare swept the Mediterranean. Christians were prevented from coming into the lands of Islam, and Moslems were not admitted to the countries of Christendom. The immense Arab empire was dominated from Baghdad by the caliph, Commander of the Faithful, both spiritual and temporal head of Islam. True, some geographical divisions soon appeared within the monolithic structure, but they were not substantial, with perhaps the exception of the minor but brilliant caliphate of Cordoba, boasting a second caliph in the far west of the empire, which had so quickly extended from Spain to India.

Europe meanwhile was almost unified under the spiritual authority of the Church headed by the pope, heir to the supremacy of Rome. The imperial authority had practically dissolved in the west. The Eastern emperor in Constantinople, the basileus, had suddenly lost most of his richer provinces to the Arabs. His main concern was to resist constant Arab pressure, and his authority was very much restricted to the formerly Greek areas of south-eastern Europe.

The frontier between Christian Europe and Islam was unstable. It was to oscillate across the Mediterranean and the southern peninsulas of Europe for many centuries. There was a frontier separating two vast territories, but the political organization on both sides (fluid and diverse in Europe, more strongly structured in Moslem regions) was headed by spiritual pontiffs, and it was the religious allegiance of the populations that made the essential difference.

Within Europe, meanwhile, many peoples in the north and the east remained pagan, and Christianization proceeded slowly—the Russian prince of Kiev, Vladimir, was baptized in 989. Among the Christians more differences, cultural, political, and liturgical appear and harden between east and west. The east remained very Greek and close to the heritage of ancient Rome. The west took on a culture in which old Latin elements mixed with powerful Germanic and Celtic components. At the court of the king of the Franks, a family descended from Charles Martel (the general who defeated the Arabs at Poitiers in 732 and pushed them back toward Spain), gained increasing influence and came to rule. Charles Martel's son, Pepin, overthrew the last Merovingian king and was elected king of France. His son, Charlemagne, became the most powerful ruler in the west: he annexed Saxony and Bavaria, then parts of North Italy, protected the pope, negotiated with the caliph Harun-al-Rashid and codified German tribal laws. On Christmas Day 800, Charlemagne was crowned emperor of the Occident by the pope in Rome. In 812 his imperial title was recognized by Byzantium, and thus the separation sharpened between east and west. No boundaries were demarcated, however, for the princes of Europe could choose and shift in their allegiance to one emperor or the other.

Charlemagne's empire did not long survive him territorially. His grandsons divided it among themselves, in three parts: the eldest, Lothair, defeated by his brothers, retained his imperial title and a central belt of territory, henceforth called Lotharingia and extending southward into Italy, as the emperor must have jurisdiction over Rome; Charles the Bald took France to the west, and Louis the German, Germany to the east. This partition was agreed upon by the Treaty of Verdun (843), the territorial clauses of which were elaborated in a lengthy conference held in Metz, still today the seat of the main bishopric of Lorraine. In most history textbooks, the mention of the Treaty of Verdun is illustrated with a map showing the division into three kingdoms of the Carolingian empire. This division laid the foundation for the territorial distribution of the various powers in that part of Europe for more than a thousand years. Indeed the political map of western Europe about 1950 can still be easily related to the frontiers drawn in 843;

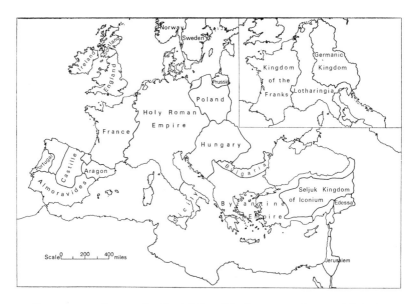

2   Europe around 1140: the Feudal Era. The inset map (*upper right*) shows the division of the Carolingian Empire by the Treaty of Verdun, 843 (see pp. 30–32).

and when the Treaty of Rome was signed in 1958 by the six participants of the European Economic Community, it seemed to reconstitute the general outline of the Carolingian realm which the Treaty of Verdun subdivided.

The conference in Metz gathered about one hundred experts, shrewd court politicians, and churchmen who, after careful study and deliberation, traced the limits of the respective realms assigned to the three brothers.[9] When tracing the frontiers, the experts gave considerable attention to the variety of resources needed by each of the three princes, and a division into territories stretching from north to south—and thus cutting across natural zones of climate and vegetation—was considered fairest and most workable. Each kingdom had a maritime façade on the North Sea, as well as one on the Mediterranean, and could therefore operate its own trans-European routes. Long discussions at Metz hinged upon the proper amount of rich farmland and of vines and orchards producing different wines and fruits, to be given to each prince. There appeared an obvious endeavor to obtain as much self-sufficiency and economic equality as possible for each territory, this situation being considered the most favorable to the maintenance of peace and good relations between the princes.

The economic factor was not the only one favoring an east-west differentiation through north-south boundaries. There were also cultural factors at work. Lothair, as the elder brother, was allowed to retain the imperial crown and with it the northern Italian territories, bordering on the Papal state around Rome (which had been granted to the Pope by Charlemagne).[10] His central position between the kingdoms of France and Germany may be interpreted as that of an arbitrator. But Lotharingia also encompassed linguistic diversity. By the time of the Treaty of Verdun the separation between the French and German languages had become quite clear, as witnessed by the records of the "Oaths of Strasbourg" in 842. The two languages still coexist nowadays in Strasbourg and in Metz. Lotharingia was to become an apple of discord between the rulers of France and Germany. It formed, particularly in its northern parts, a cultural checkerboard, perhaps largely due to its having been a border zone of the Roman Empire since Julius Caesar. Lorraine and Alsace have been disputed between France and Germany.

[9] See Roger Dion, *Les frontières de la France* (Paris, 1946); also Jean Gottmann, *A Geography of Europe* (New York, 1969), chapter 2.

[10] The Carolingian princes must have had a rather strong feeling about territorial arrangements to obtain some order and security. Pepin in 754 first donated a state to the papacy; Charlemagne confirmed, enlarged, and reorganized the donation in 781.

Belgium, Luxembourg, and the Netherlands have claimed and as-
certained independence from both, as did Switzerland and northern
Italy.

The map agreed upon at Metz and Verdun outlines territorial
patterns of great historical portent. In the early Middle Ages, carefully devised territorial settlements were exceptional. Throughout
Europe there was too much insecurity and migration of tribes, too
many local wars and roaming foreign hordes, and not enough stable
authority or law enforcement to give to a territorial entity any lasting jurisdictional value.

However, the Carolingians tried, often ruthlessly, to establish
"law and order." In 877, the edict of Guierzy rendered fiefs hered-
itary in France. Thus, the vassals of the king of France could count
on the continued authority of their descendants over the land they
held in fief. The first roots of the feudal system could hence be
planted. Still the kings were too weak and the political and social
fluidity too great immediately to give much strength to the concept
of a physical territory. Christian Europe continued for several centuries to follow to be a vaguely organized society, centered on a few
religious principles and on the allegiance of individuals to other
individuals. The continued nomadism is illustrated by the constant
incursions of the Danes into England, of the Normans into France
and Italy, of the Moslems into every country of Mediterranean
Europe, of the Swedes into various countries around the Baltic, of
the Seljuk Turks into Asia Minor, and so on. The Carolingian
dynasties fade away from the scene. Few rulers stabilized the seat of
their government in a permanent capital, besides the pope in
Rome, the basileus in Constantinople, and the caliphs in Baghdad
and Cordoba.

Two events, which might first appear as two episodes typical of
the reigning fluidity and nomadism, occurred around the long-
dreaded year 1000: the dynasty of the Capetians in France chose
Paris as its official capital and began from 987 on to organize
around that city the fiefs of the royal family; then in 1066, William,
duke of Normandy, a clever politician, invaded and conquered
England.

William the Conqueror was a powerful organizer. He was bent
on remolding the political and social structure of England: he distributed the fiefs to his Norman knights, made all vassals in England dependent on the king, and ordered the compilation of the
Domesday Book, that extraordinary inventory and assessment of all
landed property in the kingdom—one of the first economic surveys.
Under the heavy hand of William and of his successors of the

Plantagenet dynasty, England was gradually organized into one of the first solidly structured political entities of Europe. The evolution was complex, for the reigning dynasties of England and France got entangled, as a result of the lands held by the Normans and Angevins on the continent, in such a web of sovereignty, suzerainty, vassalage, and family relationships, that to extricate themselves they had to oppose one another. It took several centuries and many wars to disentangle the feudal linkages woven between the two kingdoms, but in the process the peoples affirmed their differences and their respective personalities in territories that were to be separated by the Channel and the North Sea. France and England were indeed the first among the political units of Europe to elaborate distinct state organizations on a geographical basis. Germany and Italy had inherited too much of the Roman claims to universality: after a prolonged dispute with the papacy, the German emperor Henry IV went as a penitent in 1077 to Canossa to be absolved by Pope Gregory VII—though William the Conqueror refused in 1080 to do homage as a papal vassal. But the *Dictatus Papae* in Rome (1075) had outlined the world dominance of the papacy.

Pro Patria Mori

The onslaught of "barbarian" tribes which exploded the orderly system of the Roman Empire, and was compounded from the seventh century on by the Arab Conquest, had profoundly disorganized the economic structure of the ancient world in Europe and around the Mediterranean. In the medieval period that ensued, constant migration, warfare, political instability, and piracy discouraged the gathering of the fruits of labor in certain places, if any could have been obtained beyond the bare needs of survival. The stronger royalty arising in France and England, the greater authority of the pope and the Church, the successful beginnings of great monastical orders (Cluniacs, Cistercians, Templars, and so forth) concurred from the eleventh century on to reduce insecurity and poverty in Europe. The conversion of European peoples to Christianity was practically completed, and in a few areas the Arabs and Saracens were forced to retreat. The idea of a crusade against Islam, to liberate Jerusalem, was soon to appear.

Discussing the period in English history that followed the Norman conquest, Sir Llewellyn Woodward wrote:

Throughout Europe the second half of the eleventh century and the whole of the twelfth century were periods of progress. . . . The setting of life was feudal; the general tendency was towards order. . . . Once the era of large-scale piracy and raiding had passed, some slight accumulation of capital was possible. Men were not beaten down, again and again, to the bare margin of existence. . . . The towns and cities of Europe once more gained in importance. The townsmen used the profits of trade and industry to buy privileges which ultimately proved stronger than the feudal rights of the nobles.[11]

Communities now felt strong and secure enough to invest a good deal of labor and wealth in monumental buildings. The age of the great cathedrals and abbeys began at that time, on a modest though impressive scale at first, to reach in the thirteenth to fifteenth centuries the grandeur of the Gothic cathedrals that we still admire. The cathedral held the community as if in the hands of God; its stonework, sculptures, and windows summed up in allegoric art the knowledge, history, and beliefs of the local people.[12] The community lived and died by and for the faith, in both Christian and Islamic lands.

In the political life of the medieval Christian world, however, a slow trend developed, in which the defense of the faith came to be linked to the defense of a country, of a specific portion of space, politically distinct from those adjoining it. The concept of national territory was preceded in the medieval West by an acceptance of the concept of *patria,* the fatherland, the country to which a man belongs and for the defense of which he is prepared to sacrifice his life.

The early evolution of the significance of *pro patria mori,* this basic tenet of nationalism, has been analyzed most convincingly by Ernst H. Kantorowicz.[13] In ancient Greece and Rome the words *patris* or *patria* meant "city or town of origin," and in the Middle Ages *patria* still often conveyed the meaning of home, but "the ties fettering man on earth, already slackening in the Late Empire, had lost their value." In the feudal system, a warrior could offer himself up for his lord and master: this was personal sacrifice, "resulting from the relations between lord and vassal. . . ."[14] Saint Au-

---

[11] *History of England* (London, 1962), p. 22.

[12] See especially Emile Mâle, *L'art religieux du XIIIe siècle en France* (Paris, 1925).

[13] "*Pro Patria Mori* in Medieval Political Thought," *American Historical Review,* LVI (April 1951), 472–92; elaborated again in *The King's Two Bodies* (Princeton, N.J., 1957), pp. 232–72.

[14] Kantorowicz, "*Pro Patria Mori,*" p. 477.

gustine and Abelard, however, demonstrated that Christians should do their great deeds for the love of the *patria aeterna,* the spiritual *patria,* the celestial city for which the saints had given their lives. "Heaven had become the common fatherland of the Christians."[15]

Professor Joseph R. Strayer has shown how the understanding of the basis of royal power changed in France from the twelfth to the thirteenth century: in 1124 Louis VI prayed at the abbey of Saint Denis for the defense of the kingdom and gave money to the church to obtain divine help; by 1300 Philip IV imposed taxes *ad defensionem patriae* on his people and even on the clergy.[16] The shift is notable. In the twelfth century, the Crusaders obviously fought for the faith, though the concept of *Terra Sancta,* the Holy Land, assigned to them as the target was not any longer in heaven, but an earthly piece of territory surrounding Jerusalem and Bethlehem. The references to *"la doulce France"* in the *Chanson de Roland* and other *chansons de geste* have been interpreted as references to national territory, but certainly Roland dies, fighting the Saracens, principally as a true knight for his faith and his suzerain, with just an incidental thought for the countryside at home.

Kantorowicz finds the origin of a territorial element in the *pro patria mori* ideal starting with certain sermons delivered under Philip IV of France (1285–1314) to knights leaving for the war, in which the preachers demand the supreme sacrifice for the king on the ground of the new organological concept of the state. This concept, affirmed by John of Salisbury in his *Policraticus,* will evolve to accept the extent of the realm as a *mystical body,* a manifestation of faith, for which life may be offered. Lawyers and philosophers seem to have discussed it, especially at the University of Paris, reviving some Aristotelian and Averroist principles, until by 1430, Joan of Arc could proclaim: "Those who wage war against the holy realm of France, wage war against King Jesus."

By the fifteenth century, the principle of accepting death for one's country was already strong in some parts of western Europe.[17] *Patria,* or the realm, or *respublica,* may still have been more closely associated with a community than with territory. The two, however, were beginning to mix. What is told in a few sentences and quotations, with the accumulated records of history, took in fact several centuries to evolve. For about one thousand years, since the

[15] *Ibid.,* pp. 475–76.

[16] Joseph R. Strayer, "Defence of the Realm and Royal Power in France," in *Studi in Onore di Gino Luzzatto* (Milan, 1949), pp. 289–95, and Kantorowicz, *"Pro Patria Mori,"* p. 479.

[17] Kantorowicz, *"Pro Patria Mori,"* pp. 483–90.

fourth century A.D., the thinking of Europeans had been dominated by metaphysical problems and by problems of daily, individual survival. Only in the latter part of that millenium did materialistic factors acquire enough weight in political thinking and theory to give an essential role to the territorial assets of each distinct community. The usage of the word *territorium* is more commonly found from the fourteenth century on.

The Rise of Geographical Factors

The community comes now to be discussed in terms of spatial territory, at the level of self-governing units claiming privileges of autonomy and jurisdiction. The units in medieval times were mainly cities and abbeys; they were small in area, even though they claimed jurisdiction in most cases over the lands immediately surrounding their walls. The rise of an increasing number of such communities affirming their right to self-government and therefore some freedom from the lord of the "open country" around them, required territorial delimitation, especially as the wealth and power of some of the cities grew. The story of the great cities of northern Italy and Flanders has been well studied and is generally recognized as a major factor in social fluidity and the advancement of political freedom.[18] The richer merchant classes in the cities acquired the means and the taste for education and culture, previously a monopoly of the clergy. To the formerly predominant concerns of metaphysics, religious rites, and Roman and feudal law, were added new scholarly pursuits of a more earthy nature, dealing with the human body, agricultural practices, and even geographical data.[19]

The functioning of the cities relied on more extensive relations than those of the rather localized economics of the Middle Ages. Trade had to be carried on beyond the regional frame. The Crusades opened up more horizons and routes in the Mediterranean area. The leading seaports of Italy, Genoa, Pisa, and especially

[18] See especially Henri Pirenne, *Medieval Cities: Their Origins and the Revival of Trade* (Princeton, N.J., 1925), and R. S. Lopez, *Medieval Trade in the Mediteranean World* (New York, 1950).

[19] See John K. Wright, *The Geographical Lore at the Time of the Crusades* (New York, 1925), and François de Dainville, *La géographie des humanistes* (Paris, 1940); also, E. W. Gilbert, in his Inaugural Lecture, *Geography as a Humane Study* (Oxford, 1955), has given an interesting picture of medieval geographical studies at Oxford.

Venice, had far-reaching maritime connections and even more ambitions. Venice persuaded the Fourth Crusade to go and take Constantinople in 1204 instead of waging war on the Arabs. In 1272–90, Marco Polo, a citizen of Venice, travelled through Asia to China and back. An alliance of the Flemish cities defeated the powerful king of France, Philip IV at Courtrai in 1302. In Italy the urban republics of Florence, Siena and Venice, gradually elaborated in their political life the theory and practice of political parties debating internal political matters in a way increasingly divorced from the metaphysical tradition, which inclined to let divine will decide political disputes. The French kings began also to show greater independence from the Church, especially Philip IV, whom Pope Boniface VII officially castigated in the bull *Unam sanctam* (1302). This was the time of the papacy's exile from Rome to Avignon in France.

Historians, particularly those of the German school, have usually located in France, especially during the reign of Philip IV, the appearance of the essential characteristics of the modern, centralized, national state. The kings of France did conduct, beginning with Philip Augustus (1180–1223), a rather systematic policy of gathering fiefs, at first around Paris, then in the outlying parts of the kingdom, making them direct holdings of the crown or of the royal family. In 1180 more than half of the realm of France consisted of fiefs of Henry II Plantagenet, king of England, and the king who reigned in Paris felt reduced in fact to the control of very little territory. A central position between the vast holdings of the king of England on the west and those of the emperor to the east and north gave the French king a feeling of insecurity and dissatisfaction with the feudal situation; it suggested planning for geographical expansion on the basis of nonfeudal rights. Many wars, including the Hundred Years War, and much diplomacy unfolded before France could feel it was definitely separated from the environing powers and on the way to reaching and maintaining what Cardinal Richelieu, in the seventeenth century, called her "natural frontiers" on the continent of Europe.

The situation of the country as a sort of wide isthmus in the western part of the continent between the North Sea and Channel on the one hand, and the Mediterranean Sea on the other, may have been instrumental in forcing the people living at such a disputed crossroads to organize themselves as a citadel with a strong territorial feeling. The isthmic function, already effective in Roman times and probably influential in Julius Caesar's strategy, acquired a new vitality with the Crusades, beginning with the reign of Philip Augustus.[20]

Perhaps the end of the Hundred Years War in the middle of the fifteenth century could be better understood with the temporary closing down of Mediterranean perspectives. As Joan of Arc liberated a central section of France and proclaimed the holiness of the realm in 1429–31, the Turks, scoring in the East, took Salonica in 1430 and Constantinople in 1453.[21] The Turkish Imperial Navy then dominated the Mediterranean until its defeat at Lepanto in 1571.

In the process of defending and organizing the crossroads on the isthmus, the first national state of Europe was shaped between the thirteenth and the sixteenth centuries. The role of the urban growth and power of Paris in this same period should not be underestimated. The city remained the French capital and a hub of connections binding together the various parts of the kingdom. The cosmopolitan character and early autonomy of the University of Paris, which won its independence from the king and the local bishop by 1215, obtaining a special charter from the Holy See, fostered there an early development of political theory, largely based on the ancient classics, but more conscious of historic and geographic circumstances in its interpretation of legal texts.

The close links of Paris with Rome and Italy, however, led the scholars to a concept of man-centered kingship as expressed in Dante and in Jean Bodin, with a territorially constituted state but a rather monolithic body politic. The more secure insular position of England probably allowed for the development of a more pluralistic, corporative interpretation of the crown, with less emphasis on a territory never invaded by foreign armies after 1066.[22]

If geographical factors played a significant though subtle part in the evolution of the political organization of Europe even during the Middle Ages, they assumed even greater prominence during the fifteenth century. The dominance of the Mediterranean by the Turks coincided with the coming to maturity of the kingdoms of Portugal and Spain; the latter being united by the marriage of Ferdinand of Aragon with Isabel of Castille in 1469. Under Henry

[20] See Jean Gottmann, *La politique des États et leur géographie* (Paris, 1952), especially pp. 86–88.

[21] The isthmic function in French medieval history is well argued by André Varagnac, "Pourquoi Simon de Montfort s'en alla défaire les Albigeois," in *Annales*, no. 3 (Paris, 1946), 209–18.

[22] This interpretation of medieval history is partly based on the work of Ernst H. Kantorowicz (*The King's Two Bodies*), but also on the writings of many French and British historians.

the Navigator the Portuguese, who discovered and occupied the Azores, far west in the Atlantic, in 1431–32, began rounding Africa. They reached Cape Verde in 1445 and the Gold Coast in 1482, and Diaz rounded the Cape of Good Hope in 1487. As the Portuguese settled in Angola in 1492, Columbus sailed westward to discover the West Indies.

In 1493, acting as an arbitrator between the two crowns, Pope Alexander VI divided the New World between Portugal and Spain

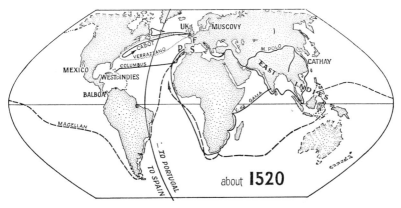

3   The Relationship of Europe to the Newly Discovered Worlds in 1520. *F*, France; *S*, Spain; *P*, Portugal; *U.K.*, England.

in the bull *Inter cetera divina* by tracing a north-south meridian line in the middle of the Atlantic. The lands east of this line would go to Portugal, while Spain would have all those to the west. The treaty of Tordesillas (1494) formalized the agreement of the two governments to that division. In 1497 Vasco da Gama sailed around the Cape and reached India in 1498. In 1499 Amerigo Vespucci discovered Venezuela, and in 1500 Cabral reached the coast of Brazil, securing it for Portugal. The accessible world was fast expanding. Cortez conquered Mexico in 1519–21, while Magellan circumnavigated the globe.

The successes of Spain and Portugal in discovering and settling new lands were indeed spectacular. The novelty and variety of these countries and their peoples created a desire for information about them that developed geographical studies. Their travels were made possible by the knowledge and new techniques that had gradually accumulated in Europe and blossomed in the Italian Renaissance of the fifteenth century. Most of the early navigators were Portuguese and Italians. The Spanish crown called on Italian captains and bankers as well as on the naval stores and credit of Antwerp to start the overseas expansion.

However, the liberal distribution of overseas territories to Spain and Portugal by the papacy, excluding the other sovereigns of Europe, did not long go unchallenged. As early as 1496, Henry VII of England gave his patronage to Cabot, a citizen of Venice, for voyages to America. Soon an Anglo-Portuguese syndicate was founded, whose ships sailed west to Newfoundland, in the part of the Atlantic officially allocated to Spain. France joined in the explorations challenging the papal division of the world. The authority of the pope and the Church was no longer as universal as it had been a few centuries earlier.

Since the end of the fourteenth century the Christian world had been seriously divided. The Great Schism was followed by a series of reformers preaching in various European countries: Wycliffe in England, John Huss in Bohemia, Savonarola in Florence. Spain had established the Inquisition. Martin Luther visited Rome in 1510; and announced his opposition to the sale of indulgences in 1517 at Wittenberg. He was excommunicated in 1520. The Reformation spread, and by 1541, when John Calvin organized the Reformed Church at Geneva and Ignatus of Loyola was elected general of the new Jesuit Order in Rome, the Christian world was deeply divided.

The great geographical discoveries concurred with the Reformation in the sixteenth century to break up the unity of political doctrine founded on the religious pillars of Roman supremacy and divine will. A new era opened up, liquidating the shifting feudal system based on personal allegiance and introducing a plurality of legal systems. The lawyers in Protestant countries felt the need to challenge the doctrinal monopoly of Roman law. Even the devout Roman Catholic lawyers in countries other than Portugal and Spain felt the need to correct the fallacy of a legal doctrine that allowed the appropriation of vast unknown spaces still to be discovered and settled.

The inner divisions of Europe and the vast potential of a new and diversified overseas world combined to require a new approach, even in legal terms, to the political appropriation of accessible space. French and British seamen began to attack Spanish ships in the Atlantic. Geographical and territorial concerns arose in the writings of jurists during the second half of the sixteenth century. Such concerns increased in the following two hundred years, establishing a link first between political sovereignty and territory, and then between a territory and the people inhabiting it.

Jean Bodin and the Variety of the World

The lawyers formed a powerful elite in the momentous debates of the sixteenth century. In Spain the leading authorities in the field, such as Francisco de Vitoria, were still stressing universal principles and the general interests of mankind as the essential concerns of public law. It was natural that the first major work stressing the sovereignty of the individual state within a partitioned and diversified world was written by a Frenchman, since France had been first in affirming her national individuality, since she was then bitterly divided by religious strife, and since she was contending with other maritime powers for the possession of newly discovered lands.[23]

Jean Bodin, born in Angers in 1520, died in Laon in 1596; in his lifetime Europeans began to colonize the wide open world, settlement developed in the Americas and in Africa, trade with the East Indies expanded, Martin Luther and John Calvin opposed pope and emperor, Michelangelo worked in Rome; the king of England, Henry VIII, established the crown's supremacy over the Church and "extinguished" papal authority in England. As Bodin began to publish (his *Methodus ad facilem historiarum cognitionem* appeared in 1566), Mercator drew his map of the world (1569), Francis Drake attacked the Spanish ports in South America (1572), Galileo was born (1564) and Raleigh discovered and annexed Virginia (1584). Two principal works by Bodin brought positivist, scientific considerations into the doctrine of public law and outlined an attempt to reconcile the facts of political geography with divine will. His work on the methodology of history and his *Les six livres de la république* (1576, French translation 1579 and 1593) are chiefly treatises on politics and law, but they insist on the variety of natural conditions amongst which human communities are scattered. Perhaps the principal purpose of any *république* (best translated into English as "commonwealth") "is to accommodate the state to the disposition of the citizen, and the edicts and ordinances to the nature of the places, people, and time." Bodin carefully describes the diversity of climatic zones on earth and relates them to the character and economic activities of the inhabitants.[24]

---

[23] See A. Bardoux, *Les légistes et leur influence sur la société française* (Paris, 1887); Adolphe Franck, *Philosophes et publicistes de l'Europe au XVIe siècle* (Paris, 1884); and Charles de Visscher, *Theory and Reality in Public International Law*, trans. P. E. Corbett (Princeton, N.J., 1957), pp. 24–31; also, J. H. Franklin, *Jean Bodin and the Sixteenth-Century Revolution in the Methodology of Law and History* (New York, 1963).

[24] Especially in Book 5 of *De la république* pp. 663–780 in the edition in

Manufacture is seen as concentrated in the northern countries of Europe, while the southern peoples are of a more contemplative nature and therefore more inclined toward science, philosophy, and religion. The diversity of the various parts of the world leads to a division of labor among them, from which ensue international trade and interdependence.

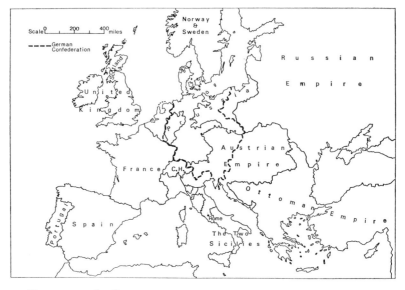

4   Europe around 1560.

Bodin describes with many examples the complementarity of the different parts of the global system and undertakes to demonstrate that such are the products of providential planning. For the good of the whole of mankind, God did not give to any single people enough qualities and resources to make them independent. In another work, answering the "paradoxes" of M. de Malestroit on economic theory (1568), Bodin becomes an advocate of international trade, which he considered a consequence of and a cure for the diversity and inequalities of the various countries.[25]

French published in Lyon 1593. See also the English translation by Richard Knolles, *The Six Bookes of a Commonweale* (London, 1606), ed. Kenneth D. McRae (Cambridge, Mass., 1962).

[25] Jean Bodin's *Réponse aux paradoxes de M. de Malestroit touchant l'enchérissement de toutes les choses et des monnaies* (Paris, 1568 and Lyon,

Despite his insistence on interdependence, Bodin is neither a true liberal nor a champion of free trade. He is quite conscious of the need for the state to be independent and strongly organized. The country must be protected, and tariff barriers may well be part of the political organization of international cooperation, for they must be a prerogative of national authority. In the history of political theory, Bodin is known for his advocacy of a strong, almost absolutist form of government, preferably a monarchy. The title of his concluding work, *De la république,* may cause some misunderstanding in modern terminology, which opposes *monarchy* and *republic.* In sixteenth century Latin, *respublica* meant "the political community," as in the Latin version of Plato's *Republic.* Bodin stressed the political partitioning of space into separate units, each of which ought to be a strong realm. Perhaps Machiavelli's *Prince* influenced him in certain respects.[26] But Bodin was deeply interested in resources, economics, and complementarity between the various countries of the world.

While emphasizing complementarity, Bodin advocated authoritarian central power in the state to insure the freedom and independence of the nation as a whole. A Roman Catholic lawyer living in a time and a country torn by bitter religious strife, Bodin could not be a defender of individual freedom, but he favored a nation's freedom to participate in the concert of nations. From the beginning of his *République* he states that the commonwealth is endowed with sovereignty and that sovereignty must be maintained, if necessary in God's name. He hints at the advantage in every sect's having a separate state, anticipating the treaties of Westphalia in 1648.

The transition from the medieval universality founded on the unity of faith to the coexistence of a multiplicity of sovereign states based on the diversity of geography and of religion is quite obvious in the whole work of Bodin. Much of his reasoning and some of his geography was borrowed from Plato, Herodotus, and Aristotle as well as more recent sources. The advocacy of active international trade is certainly anti-Platonic and reflects the thirst for geographical opportunity in a century of great discoveries and explorations.

1593) is a rather advanced economic theory of fighting inflation through international trade. The principle is already affirmed in his *Méthode* (chapter 3), and later again in his *République.* The economic and geographical theories of Jean Bodin have been well reported and analyzed by Pierre Dockès, *L'espace dans la pensée économique du XVIᵉ au XVIIIᵉ siècle* (Paris, 1969), pp. 79–98.

[26] Machiavelli died in 1527, but his writings must have been discussed by the teachers and colleagues of Jean Bodin.

Some lines of the *Method* announce the slogan publicized by the I.B.M. Corporation in the 1940s: "World peace by world trade." Of the new world emerging on the horizon, Bodin had learnt a good deal, and he used the available geographic information, supplementing it with the classics. The tradition that leads to Hobbes and Montesquieu begins here. Bodin emphasizes the sovereign's need to know as much as possible about the people, land, and resources within the territory under his jurisdiction, as well as about those of neighboring lands.[27] He believes in the ultimate benefits of migration and knows that some of the shortcomings of natural conditions in a given region may be compensated by human labor and art.

The sixteenth century indeed opened a new era in European thought about politics and about the environment. One of the essential innovations lay in the realization that the rapidly expanding accessible world needed a new organization geared to national identity and international cooperation. Greater affluence resulting from the influx of the gold and silver of the New World and the expansion of trade supported the trend.

The Treaties of Westphalia, 1648.

The liquidation of the feudal and religious system of the Middle Ages was accelerated by the great geographical discoveries. The new territories drew large numbers of people from Europe either to settle or to engage in seafaring activities linking Europe with these distant lands. From these lands in turn came many products, among them gold and silver from America, that swelled the flow of economic activities and intra-European migration.

The extraordinary abundance of money that developed in Europe caused rapid urban growth and industrial expansion. Land and agriculture ceased being the all-important economic resources, and people could not be kept on the land, producing harvests for their lords. As Spaniards and Portuguese sailed overseas, a great demand for manpower developed in those countries, and French laborers escaped to Spain by the tens of thousands, taking advan-

---

[27] In Book 6, chapter 1 of *De la république*, Bodin advises government to conduct population and economic censuses within the country: "Census, en bons termes, n'était rien autre chose que l'estimation des biens d'un chacun . . . et si la nécessité y est évidente, encore est l'utilité plus grande, soit pour entendre le nombre et qualité des personnes, soit pour l'estimation et déclaration des biens d'un chacun, soit pour régler et morigéner les sujets."

tage of greater opportunities in the richer country. Portugal imported some Negro manpower from Africa. The Spanish and Portuguese crowns, indebted to the merchants of Antwerp, who supplied most of the timber and naval stores needed for maritime expansion, sent the spices from the East Indies and the gold and silver brought back by the galleons to Antwerp for repayment. Venetian bankers moved to Antwerp and Brussels to take advantage of the new business boom of the Low Countries. Antwerp assumed a role somewhat similar to that of New York in the twentieth century. Naturally the merchants of Antwerp, Brussels, and Ghent refused to follow the Netherlands to the north in the struggle for independence from the Hapsburgs and Spain.

The Hapsburgs were obtaining credit from bankers elsewhere, too, and the Fugger banking family of Augsburg, in feudal fashion, was given Venezuela to exploit to regain some of the borrowed money. The French kings, meanwhile, had a close alliance with the Medici family, perhaps the greatest banking house of the time; and two queens of France, Catherine de Medici and Marie de Medici, had great power in Europe from 1550 to 1620. The general tableau of European politics and economics in 1600 would have seemed unbelievable to an educated man of the fifteenth century. Entirely new problems and concepts of economics had become central concerns of government.

The greatest change, however, was in that same period the deep spiritual revival that broke up the religious unity of Christian Europe and plunged most of it into a series of devastating wars, some of which were civil wars and international conflicts simultaneously.

In that troubled time of warfare Europeans suffered greatly on the continent. In the Thirty Years War Germany lost about one third of her total population. People yearned for security. It had become obvious that a new system of political organization was needed, and the seventeenth century saw the beginnings of it. The outdated inheritance of Roman universality had to be formally repealed at a time when a divided Europe was asserting world supremacy in a pluralistic system. The legal instruments of Roman inheritance were shelved for all practical purposes as a result of the Treaties of Westphalia signed on 24 October 1648. At about the same time, the first principles of what has become international public law were formulated. The granting of equal rights of territorial sovereign jurisdiction to all states was a basic prerequisite of such a body of law. Each state that had full freedom of action within its own territory could agree to deal on an equal basis, as an independent participant, in a scheme of international relations. As in most matters relating to diplomatic negotiations, many of the clauses of the Westphalia Peace documents of 1648 could be interpreted in rather different ways. It is not my intention here to give an analysis of the text, a task that has been attempted in detail by many jurists and historians. The conclusions of the various studies concur on the major aspects of the matter we are concerned with. The treaties of Munster and Osnabrück were prepared by long conferences in which all the important European states except England, Poland, and Russia were represented.

The treaties formally recognized the then well-established independence of Switzerland and the Netherlands from the Holy Roman Empire.[28] The two countries that then attained full territorial sovereignty were indeed "nations" rather than kingdoms, both with confederal internal structures. The Dutch representative signed for the "Estates General of the Netherlands" and not for the prince of Orange, their *stadhouder*. The treaties also gave to Sweden large possessions within German territory along the Baltic. These acquisitions established Sweden as the dominant power in the Baltic area; they also made Sweden a participant in the Holy Roman Empire, with votes for her German territories in the Imperial Diet.

The dispositions excluding Switzerland and the Netherlands from the Holy Roman Empire and granting membership to Sweden because of land acquisition in Germany show that the empire had for all practical purposes accepted a limited and variable territorial delimitation and had renounced the old claims to general dominance in Europe. In fact, the Peace of Westphalia grants actual territorial sovereignty to all the princes of the empire and confirms the privileges and territorial jurisdictions of the Free Cities. This established about three hundred sovereignties within the empire, many of them too small to survive. The result was to reduce to vague legal and diplomatic claims the political function of the emperor over the whole territorial extent of the empire, that is, of the areas represented in the diet. The actual sovereign jurisdiction of the emperor was thus restricted to territory over which he could claim sovereignty from other sources than the imperial crown.

Modifying still further the nature of the Holy Roman Empire, traditionally linked to the Church of Rome, the treaties of West-

---

[28] Swiss tradition traces the independence of Switzerland to the defensive league formed between Uri, Schwyz, and Unterwalden against imperial authority on 1 August 1291; by 1513 the league included thirteen member cantons, the same number as in 1648.

phalia guaranteed toleration to the three major Christian religions of Europe (Catholic, Calvinist, and Lutheran). The toleration, however, was to be granted in each country by its sovereign ruler, and the sovereign's religion was to be the official religion of the state. The famous formula imposing a state religion, *"Cujus regio illius religio,"* may be interpreted in different ways: on one hand it admitted the fact of Protestant powers, even within the framework of the Holy Roman Empire; on the other hand it attempted to freeze the geographic distribution of the respective religions in Europe along the lines of the 1648 situation. A clause even dictated that a prince would forfeit his right to rule if he were to change his religion. This clause has been interpreted by some as an attempt to limit the spread of Protestantism, but it may also be considered a safeguard for the religion predominant at any given time in a country, and presumably the same as that of the prince, so that the majority could not lose their privileges because of a ruler's change of mind.

Tolerance of the minority's religion was thus left at the discretion of the government in every state, though guaranteed in principle. In many countries the guarantee did not last long, but the Peace laid down the foundation of a pluralistic religious, political, and social system in Europe, repealing the monolithic theories of a long past. Sovereignty was to be exercised within definite territorial boundaries. Personal allegiance to the prince was removed as the basis of political organization. Sovereignty was still associated with inheritance and with religion, but with more choice and variation than in any of the past arrangements.

Somewhere behind the treaties themselves an optimistic analyst finds there recognition of a link between territorial sovereignty and the will of the majority of the territory's population. The obvious relationship between sovereignty and effective settlement of territory will be fully established only in the eighteenth century, particularly by the treaties recognizing the independence of the United States. But the treaties of 1648 may be considered as a prologue.

The Treaty of Münster, which Spain and the Netherlands signed in 1648, went beyond making arrangements for Europe. It mentioned possessions overseas, including areas where Spanish and Dutch maritime expansion met and mixed. One such area was on the other side of the globe, in the Pacific Ocean, and had been reached first by the Portuguese when Magellan circumnavigated the globe. By 1565 the Spaniards reached and conquered the Philippines while the Portuguese established themselves in the Moluccas and on the island of Celebes. Early in the seventeenth century

the Dutch East India Company was operating in that sector of the
Pacific, and the Dutch ejected the Portuguese from the Moluccas
by 1615, founded Batavia on Java in 1619, and landed in Formosa
in 1635. They were also competing with the Portuguese for the
trade with Japan. The treaty of Münster had to deal with an area
of possible conflict between the Netherlands and Spain over Pacific
islands in the Far East.

It is interesting that one of the documents on the acquisition of
territorial sovereignty most quoted in recent years, the arbitration
by Judge Max Huber in the *Island of Palmas* case (1928) had to do
with a small isolated island, located in the Pacific between Min-
danao (Philippines), Celebes, and the Moluccas. The sovereignty
of the island was disputed between the United States and the
Netherlands in the beginning of the twentieth century. The United
States claim was based on the treaty of 1898 by which Spain ceded
the Philippines, and the Treaty of Münster of 1648 had to be
brought into the discussion before the arbitrator.[29] As a result of
the rapid expansion of the west European maritime powers around
the globe, the Peace of Westphalia could not limit itself to the continent of Europe. The politics of Europe were already embroiled
with problems of sovereignty over other accessible parts of the
world.

To a large extent the Treaties of Westphalia merely agreed to
recognize and legalize a situation already established *de facto* for
some time. Their ratification, however, supplied a new pattern of
political organization, now formally accepted, for the relations between peoples. It was a much more pluralistic organization than it
had ever been since Roman law and order had become prevalent.
The hierarchical structure culminating at the Holy See and the
Holy Roman Empire had been terminated and replaced by a multiplicity of territorial sovereignties and even of beliefs. No wonder
the papacy protested in 1651 against the ratification of the treaties.
No wonder that the date of 1648, and various clauses in the treaties,
have been often cited as marking the advent of a new political and
legal order in Europe, one arranged around the fundamental unit
of the national state endowed with territorial sovereignty.

The Purposes of Territorial Sovereignty

Once acquired, sovereignty has been treasured and defended by
every nation as its most valuable possession, and it has been based

[29] See p. 4, note 5.

on the control of a territory. As the concept of a corporate national sovereignty gradually replaced the personal prerogatives of the individual sovereign,[30] territorial delimitation acquired much more significance: it fixed limits to the spatial extent of sovereignty and outlined the size and location of it. The territory became the physical and legal embodiment of national identity, and the jurists and philosophers of the seventeenth century began to discuss how sovereign governments ought to use these prerogatives. There is little doubt about the main doctrine that prevailed. Charles de Visscher emphasizes that both Hobbes and Spinoza, though conditioned by different backgrounds, agreed on the need for strong central authority to provide security to the country and to the individuals within it. Security was the dominant wish, and it became the major purpose of sovereignty.[31]

Between nations, the law of nature would lead to the rule of force in Hobbes's understanding of the world, and Spinoza saw sovereign states moved only by uncontrolled self-interest. The concept of sovereignty that emerged was, therefore, a rather negative one based on the authority and exclusivism of the state within the established territorial frame. Jurists concerned themselves with the major question of how to regulate the behavior of the people in the territory over which the sovereignty applied. Most of them contributed more to the psychological lore of their time, as Hobbes certainly did, and to the permanent debate over basic moral issues, than to the idea of improving the lot of the people by developing the economy of the territory. Economic planning began to be discussed, however, at that time.

Among the possible purposes of sovereignty, the emphasis remained on security. Indeed it was a rare and much-needed commodity at a time of bitter religious strife, of dynastic intrigues, of revolutions and inquisition, of almost constant warfare throughout Europe. Invited by Louis XIV to Paris in 1665 for advice on a new design for the Louvre and on the replanning of central Paris, the great Roman architect Bernini wrote in a memorandum to the king that the time might be well suited for large-scale plans because the realm was enjoying that very unusual thing, a period of peace![32]

The overwhelming concern for security led to a restrictive inter-

---

[30] See especially the interesting theory of Ernst H. Kantorowicz in *The King's Two Bodies*, placing the emergence of the crown as a permanent corporate concept in Elizabethan England.

[31] Charles de Visscher, *Theory and Reality*, pt. 1, ch. 1.

[32] Jean Gottmann, *Essais sur l'aménagement de l'espace habité* (Paris, 1966), pp. 200–201; see also Steen Eiler Rasmussen, *Towns and Buildings* (Liverpool, 1956).

pretation of the purposes of territorial sovereignty. This interpretation has been with us for some three hundred years. By the sovereignty and equality of states the international lawyer nowadays means, as Ian Brownlie put it,

(1)   a jurisdiction, *prima facie* exclusive, over a territory and the permanent population living there;
(2)   a duty of non-intervention in the area of exclusive jurisdiction of other states;
(3)   the dependence of obligations arising from customary law and treaties on the consent of the obligor.[33]

For the constitutional lawyer, sovereignty means the responsibility of having the constitutional laws of state drawn, accepted, and enforced to insure the functioning of the country in the public interest. The pursuit of the public interest is basically interpreted also in the restrictive terms of attending to legislation, regulation, and administration. To assure security, sovereignty finds itself usually seeking order, and only seldom considering change.

One can hardly miss the consistency of the thought that leads from Plato's *Laws* to Hobbes and to the classic interpretation of sovereignty by many twentieth-century lawyers. They see it as a large sign reading "keep off these grounds," posted on territorial limits. They do not see it as actually concerned with securing the "good life," unless that expression merely means "peace and order." This does not imply in the legal concept of sovereignty an attitude necessarily restricting international trade or discouraging foreign trade. But when a choice between security and opportunity for the people must be made, this school of thought would always prefer security, and it feels security constantly and dangerously threatened by the lure of opportunity.

Such was not, however, the opinion of all the great lawyers, even in the sixteenth and seventeenth centuries. Jean Bodin, sometimes cited as the father of the idea of national sovereignty, was certainly dissenting from the classic Platonic principle; he welcomed, even on moral grounds, the variety of the world and the necessary complementarity of its diverse parts. One may venture to say that Bodin saw the territorial sovereignty of every state as a *prerequisite* to adapting its system of laws to the geographical circumstances and to the character of the people. This adaptation should be achieved in order to prepare the state better to become a worthy and willing

[33] Ian Brownlie, *Principles of Public International Law* (Oxford, 1966), p. 250.

participant in an international system cemented by active general trade.[34] In the early seventeenth century another eminent lawyer, the Dutchman Huig de Groot or Grotius, is often credited with the paternity of international law. He lived and worked in the time of Shakespeare, Bacon, Raleigh, Richelieu, Descartes, and Galileo. His first important work, *Mare liberum* (written in 1604, published in 1609) was at first considered a pamphlet upholding the right of the Dutch to navigation and commerce on the high seas despite Portuguese or Spanish claims to monopoly. English lawyers saw in it an attack on English claims to the "sovereignty of the British seas," considered necessary to the security of the British Isles, and John Selden produced an exhaustive work, *Mare clausum,* in reply. But Grotius had placed the principle of the freedom of the high seas in the forefront of international law, and he did so in the formative years of the law, when geographical discovery by sea was an essential endeavor and the expansion of overseas trade a primary feature of European opportunity.[35] His much-quoted sentences set forth more than the maritime law: he pointed out that whatever could not be seized or enclosed could not be made a subject of property:

The vagrant waters of the ocean are thus necessarily free. The right of occupation, again, rests upon the fact that most things become exhausted by promiscuous use and that appropriation consequently is the condition of their utility to human beings. But this is not the case with the sea; it can be exhausted neither by navigation nor by fishing, that is to say, in neither of the two ways in which it can be used.[36]

It is interesting to observe that the law of the sea was first to link sovereignty obviously and forcefully with opportunity; Plato's dislike of maritime influences was rightly consistent with his craving for security and order. But more important was that as Grotius showed, territorial sovereignty over certain kinds of space could coexist with the freedom of other sectors. Finally, the appropriation of sovereignty over territory ought to be considered, like the property of so many objects, as a function of the uses of that territory by people. One of the purposes suggested for sovereignty and inter-

[34] See above, pp. 41–44.
[35] C. John Colombos, *The International Law of the Sea,* 6th ed. (London, 1968), especially pp. 56–65.
[36] Grotius, *Mare liberum,* as quoted by Colombos, pp. 62–63. Some aspects of this passage take on a curious note in the context of the modern concern with the pollution of the environment.

national organization was constructive rather than restrictive: promoting usefulness to people.

Sovereignty had been interpreted too often as a function of the regulation of power, and especially political power. In the administration of territory, however, sovereignty had to deal with economic resources and services, with the management of ways of life, and with improvement and development as well as with regulation, limitation, and prevention. The sovereign's duties and responsibilities had been essentially political, religious, and military until the sixteenth century (though such had not always been the policy of the rulers of Greek cities and certainly not of Alexander the Great and some of the Caesars). With an expanding world opening up before a rising number of sovereign states, new purposes of government were coming to the fore in the economic realm. The characteristics of territory and their use were acquiring a new significance.

III

Liberty versus Equality:
The Competition for Progress

IN THE seventeenth century political philosophy came to realize the need to free the evolution of nations from old shackles. The privileges of sovereignty were claimed by an increasing number of nations, whose aims were, first, to take into their own hands the responsibility for their security, and second, to organize their territory for their own use and comfort.

Opportunity had become, next to security, a normal aspiration of political communities. Territory was now to be administered not only as a shelter, a portion of inhabited space protected by a "Great Wall" (actually erected around most cities), but also as a receptacle of the economic means of the people. Among these means had to be counted the population itself, the agricultural potential of the land, the useful mineral deposits, the streams and inland lakes, the fauna of the coastal waters, the cattle, the industries and skills of the cities, and the profits from foreign trade. The European economy had grown beyond the stage of local self-sufficiency based on agricultural production, which had been the rule for most lands (except a few trading cities) in the Middle Ages. The advent of money management, of larger industries, and of capitalism brought the central government not only to tax, levy tolls, and spend, but also to invest. How much economic regulation should the sovereign be allowed? Most of the European states were passing through a period of absolute or at least very authoritarian regimes, as was the case even in England under Cromwell and after. Hobbes's *Leviathan* was not out of tune with the political thought of the seventeenth century as a whole. The famous sentence ascribed to Louis XIV, *"L'Etat, c'est moi,"* testifies to the increasing centralization of political power, and this required the sovereign to exercise economic power as well.

Economic power, as shown in the writings of Adolf A. Berle, is "power without glory."[1] Although wielded by individuals, it results from the control of an organization. It has a collective structure, and rests on a network of material connections. The nature of economic power expresses itself in a definite spatial form; several dis-

[1] Adolf A. Berle, *Power* (New York, 1969), especially pp. 143-73.

tinct forms of economic power may coexist in the same space, but each has, at a given time, definite geographical boundaries. Political or spiritual power may rest on the psychology of people; economic power needs material expression. *Economics* was a word formed from the Greek root *oikos,* meaning "house," the original unit of man's organization of space.[2]

The emergence of territorial concern in the philosophy of economic organization coincided with the rapid expansion, from the sixteenth century on, of new land to be appropriated outside Europe, and also with the growth of resources due to the development of commerce, industry, and banking. It seems paradoxical that, as instruments of wealth *other* than tilled land multiplied, interest developed in a territorial base of political organization. This trend, however, may not be paradoxical at all if one admits that territorial fractioning of sovereignty was necessary to increase the number of sovereign units competing freely for their share in the new wealth. Territorial sovereignty became in the seventeenth century, and remains, the foundation of a certain status of equality between states, like that which must exist between sovereigns.

It was also a *de jure*—if not always a *de facto*—guarantee of freedom of economic planning as well as religious policy within each state. With the spread of territorial sovereignty, economic policy needed a doctrine, and the history of economic thought has classified this period as the "era of mercantilism." The mercantilists gave much attention to the use of territory; this was often misunderstood for an emphasis on land for agricultural production. In fact, the early period of sovereignty opened the door for some freedom in competing for more opportunity. The regulation of this new freedom and of competition within the respective states gradually caused the labor of the people to be considered a nation's essential resource.

The Territory as a Source of Wealth

Until the Renaissance, economic power in Europe had been able to concentrate wealth in four main forms: the most widespread form was the control of the yield of the land, for food was the

---

[2] From the same root was formed the word *ecology* to describe the study of living organisms in relation to the natural conditions of their habitat; ecology is intertwined with geographical distribution. Recently, the Greek architect and planner, C. A. Doxiadis, coined the word *ekistics* to describe the study of human settlements.

condition of survival; the second form was the tollhouse located on a road, or at a gate, or even better, at a crossroads, controlling passage; a third form was a monopoly privilege to produce or market a given commodity; the fourth form was the privilege of minting money thus manipulating at will means of payment. Each of these forms of wealth could not exist, amidst medieval insecurity, without proper political and military protection, which had to be provided by the lord himself or his suzerain. All the four forms of wealth rested on some clear spatial basis: ownership of the land, gathering of tolls, enforcing monopolistic rights, of which minting money was one. Each of these had to be located in specific areas and places, and rights were exercised within certain geographic boundaries, though the latter could shift in time. There was a territorial substratum and definition to each of these resources. Taxation was applied mainly in the form of fees and tolls; it was largely supplemented by servitudes paid to the lord or his agent in kind or in labor. Credit was little used, and the manipulation of money, which was to become plentiful in the sixteenth and seventeenth centuries, was hardly a basis of economic power unless the sovereign himself, who minted money, engaged in it. This was demonstrated in practice by various kings, especially by Philip IV of France, when he banished successively the Lombards, the Jews, and the Templar Knights, all money managers in his time, in order to confiscate their assets in his kingdom. He also modified several times, at will, the metal content or exchange value of his coins.

The sources of wealth in those times were, therefore, based on monopolistic privilege applying in a place or area. If the density of monopolies in a certain area grew very thick, it might cause a slackening of local activities stifled by so many controls and fees.

These economic structures were not peculiar to Europe alone nor to the Middle Ages exclusively. Inhabited space has always been so used for gathering wealth produced by the labor or trade of the population. These various forms of wealth existed in the ancient civilizations, and to a large extent they are still with us in various aspects of contemporary economic institutions, private or public.

Government concerned itself with economic policies quite early. The *Iliad* tells the story of the Greeks' war to take Troy, a great, rich, and proud city, which stood at the crossroads of the Dardanelles Straits, at the gate of the Pont. Although the epic does not insist on the economic and territorial motives behind the Trojan War, it does mention the wealth of Troy, and the Homeric hymn to Delian Apollo (see above, pp. 22–23), stresses economic consideration.

Location appears early as a basic asset of territory for its own people as well as for outsiders.[3] Natural or artificial assets of location are expressed in the tollhouse or market functions of the place. But a strongly organized control of the population's activities soon emerges as the sovereign's usual way to gather the economic means of exercising the powers conferred by sovereignty. Hellenistic Egypt, under the Ptolemaic dynasty, offers one of the best known examples of complete monopolistic dominance of a country's economy by the central authority. Describing it in a classic work, the Russian emigré historian Michael Ivanovich Rostovtzeff could hardly avoid comparing this ancient version of economic *étatism* to the Soviet economic system under Stalin's rule.[4] Technological progress caused substantial differences in social structure, but government monopoly applied in rather similar fashion to all sectors of economic activity.

The Romans gave more freedom to individual initiative and encouraged competition within the framework of their laws and taxation. In the Middle Ages the ability of government to tax was weakened by the fractioning of political authority, general insecurity, and the shrinking of the generation of wealth. Stronger territorial sovereignty and more sedentarization had to develop before rulers or assemblies could start gathering substantial financial proceeds from their people. To find out what the resources were, some surveying was first needed, and the Domesday Book has been rightly revered as an early model for this method.[5]

The economic dilemma over the use of territory is perhaps best illustrated by the debate, famous in Chinese history, that went on in the council of Genghis Khan when the Mongol emperor conquered western China (1211–15). Coming from the dry ranges of the Mongolian steppes, the conquerors were surprised by the economy of China, a more humid, diversified, densely populated, and intensively cultivated country. As the Chinese chronicler tells it:

When Chinghiz [Genghis] invaded the western countries [of China], he did not have in his stores a single measure of rice or a single yard of silk. When [they came to the Chinese provinces] his advisers said, "Although you have now conquered the men of Han, they are no use to us; it would be better to kill them all and turn the lands back to pasture so that we

[3] See Jean Gottmann, *La politique des États et leur géographie* (Paris, 1952), pp. 70–120.

[4] *Social and Economic History of the Hellenistic World* (Oxford, 1941); also C. Préaux, *L'économie royale des Lagides* (Brussels, 1939).

[5] See H. C. Darby et al., *The Domesday Geography of England*, 5 vols. (Cambridge, England, 1952–67).

can feed our beasts on it.". . . But Yehlü said, "Now that you have conquered everywhere under Heaven and all the riches of the four seas, you can have anything you want, but you have not yet organized it. You should set up taxation on land and merchants, and should make profits on wine, salt, iron, and the produce of the mountains and marshes. In this way in a single year you will obtain 500,000 ounces of silver, 80,000 rolls of silk, and 400,000 piculs of grain. How can you say that the Chinese people are no use to you?"[6]

The first adviser was true to Mongol tradition: the essential instruments of wealth to him were pastures and the horses and cattle on the range. The second adviser suggested a diversification of investment: to the usual resources, plentifully available to the Mongols, he wanted to add grain, silk, and silver. His opinion prevailed; Genghis Khan agreed to a program of taxation, and his successors perfected it to a remarkable extent. Few regimes imposed a system of taxes as crushing and all-pervading as the Mongol dynasty did in China. It was the overwhelming burden of taxation that ultimately provoked the rebellion of the Chinese people.

Territory has no economic value in itself; it generates wealth in many different ways as a result of the uses to which it is put by its inhabitants. Listening to Ye-lü Ch'u-tsai (or Jehlü) advising Genghis Khan, one perceives the elements of the economic thinking that will, centuries later, proclaim with Adam Smith and Karl Marx that the wealth of a nation is the labor of its people.[7] However, people and territory are not separable in the production of goods and services: production must occur somewhere, and the place or area is one of the conditioning factors of the economic process. The territory where the process develops must be under a political régime, within a given system of laws, and at a certain location with respect to means of transport and markets. The territory, being the habitat of the people, is the receptacle of its economic activities. It was only in the seventeenth century that economic and political thought in Europe began to realize this significance of territory.

Territory, Population, and Taxation

Marshal Sebastien Le Prestre de Vauban (1633–1707) is often considered the father of modern military engineering, but he was also

---

[6] Hsü Thung Chien Kang Mu, Chap. 19, p. 276, as quoted by Joseph Needham, *Science and Civilization in China* (Cambridge, England, 1954), I, 140 (Needham's interpolations) .

[7] See the opening statement of Adam Smith's *Wealth of Nations* (1776) and the central theory of Karl Marx in *Das Kapital* (1867) .

deeply interested in economics. Through some of his writings he
became a notable forerunner of modern economists, geographers,
and planners even in their endeavors to make long-range forecasting.[8] His most important economic work is a memorandum submitted to king Louis XIV about 1700, suggesting the establishment
of a single tax, proportionate to the income of each subject and
paid by all. The French treasury was then in a sorry state, and
Vauban sought to demonstrate that the tax he outlined would yield
the revenue desired to implement the king's policies. He felt that
the masses were poor and the country's resources inadequately developed chiefly because of the oppressive and unequal system of
taxation then in force. His project was rejected by the cabinet and
the king, but Vauban had an elaborate edition of his plan printed
for private circulation under the title *Projet d'une dixme royale . . .*
In 1708 a translation appeared in London under the title *A Project
for a Royal Tythe: or General Tax*.[9] A second English edition in
1710 seems to have been submitted to the House of Commons.

From the very beginning Vauban stressed a few points still basic
in geography and in economics:

When I say that France is the finest Kingdom in the World, I tell no
News, for that has been own'd a long time; but if I should add that it
is the richest, nobody will believe it by what they see. It is nevertheless
an evident Truth, and one may easily be convinced of it, if they will
but consider, that it is not great heaps of Gold and Silver that make
Kingdoms great and rich; there being vast Countries in the World that
abound in those, and yet have neither Plenty nor Happiness. Such as
Peru, and several other kingdoms of *America,* and of the *East* and *West-
Indies,* which abound in Gold and Precious Stones, and yet want Bread.
The true Riches of a Kingdom, consist in the abundance of such Goods,
as are of necessary use for the Support of Men's Lives, and which they
cannot be without. . . . For it is a Truth beyond all contradiction, That

8 See Jean Gottmann, "Vauban and Modern Geography," *Geographical Review,* XXXIV (1944), 120–28; and Henry Guerlac, in E. M. Earle et al.,
Makers of Modern Strategy (Princeton, N.J., 1943), pp. 26–48. Among the better biographies of Vauban: Daniel Halevy, *Vauban* (Paris, 1923); P. Lazard,
Vauban (Paris, 1937); Sir Reginald Blomfield, *Sébastien Le Prestre de Vauban*
(London, 1938), and also a bibliography by Capitaine Gazin, *Essai de bibliog-
raphie: oeuvres concernant Vauban* (Paris, 1933).

9 *A Project for a Royal Tythe: or General Tax; which, By suppressing all the
Ancient Funds and Later Projects for Raising the Publick Revenues, and for
ever abolishing all Exemptions, unequal Assessments, and all rigorous and oppressive Distraining on the People, will furnish the Government a Fixt and
Certain Revenue, sufficient for all its Exigencies and Occasions, without op-
pressing the Subjects. By the Famous Monsieur Vauban, Marshal of France,
Knight of the King's Orders, and Governour of Lisle* (London: John Matthews,
1708).

the best Soil differs in nothing from the worst, if it is not cultivated. This Cultivating becomes not only useless, but destructive, both to the Master and Tenant, by reason of the charges he is obliged to be at upon it, if, for want of Consumption, the Product of his Land lies on his hand for want of a Merchant.[10]

Here the discussion of what constitutes a natural resource is directly tied up with the problem of consumption, with the principle of supply and demand. The first part of this memorandum to the crown is devoted to a survey of the existing situation, appraising the agricultural production, the urban economy, and the regular revenues of the government. Vauban shows that the existing system of taxes and tariffs deprives peasants and merchants of adequate profits. Then in the second part, he introduces a project of fiscal reform. He stresses the aim of simultaneously enriching sovereign and subjects, thereby strengthening both king and country. He dares point out that the sovereign needs his subjects as much as they need him. Knowing more about the numbers and ways of life of his people would be to the king's advantage, "since it is certain, that the Preservation and Increase of his People, is his chief and principal Interest, and that their Misery and Ruine is the greatest Mischief that can befal him."

To assess a general tax and plan economic policies, it is necessary first to survey fully the whole territory and the population inhabiting it. In his seventh chapter, Vauban attempts an evaluation of the area of France ("Measur'd according to the best and latest Maps") and of a "List of the People." The latter is the oldest known scientific estimate of the French population, and an ancestor of modern censuses.[11] In chapter ten, Vauban returns to the need for censuses and surveys made at regular intervals; he gives models of "formularies," or questionnaires, and of tables to record the population of each parish and its characteristics. He used such questionnaires and tables in his own studies of two provinces, one rich (the "Election" of Rouen in Normandy), and one poor ("Election" of Vézelay in Burgundy), as samples of his method.

Would it not, further, be an extream Pleasure to him the King, to run over, in his Closet, and in the space of one hour, the present and past State of that great Kingdom of which he is Soveraign; and to see and know perfectly, by himself, wherein his Grandeur, his Riches and his Strength consist? To see plainly the Happiness or Misery of his People;

---

[10] Vauban, *op. cit.*, quoted from the 1708 edition.

[11] Vauban's estimate of the total population of France in 1699–1700 was 19,904,146 inhabitants, a figure recognized to have been very close to the reality.

he Significance of Territory

and how to promote the one and remedy the other? . . . But to make them [the surveys] the more Compleat, and perfectly Intelligible, there might be added Plans and Maps of the Towns and Countries, so Carefully and Particularly done, as that all the Woods, Meadows and arable Ground, Rivers, Rivulets, Marshes, Mountains, Hills, Castles, Villages, Abbies, Farms, Mills, Bridges, Roads, etc., should be distinguished by their Names and Figures, and placed at their true distance from each other, upon the Maps; which should be drawn Geometrically and fairly; which might be done by means of a *French Atlas,* divided into so many Books as there are Provinces in France.

One can well see what good use Vauban would have made of modern data banks and computers. His wish for a good French atlas, with all details mapped upon it, took more than two hundred years to materialize.[12] The emphasis on the need for geographical data on which to base policies and economic planning was, of course, fully accepted by 1900 in the more advanced countries. Vauban pointed out that the relationship between government (or the sovereign) and the people must be implemented in terms of the spatial organization of the territory. Even the assessment of a general tax requires that such economic factors as land use, land ownership, agricultural production, distribution of population, urban and rural settlements, industrial plants, means of transport and communication, as well as many variable characteristics of each of these aspects of the territory, be taken into account.

Understood in this wider sense, encompassing its economic and physical features and organization, territory becomes the basic set of factors linking government to population. In the tripartite formula of the modern state, territory is the *essential constant* linking the people to the unified governmental structure. The economic relationships between people and territory on one hand, and between government and territory on the other, will constantly vary according to a multifaceted set of factors among which available technology, as well as available knowledge about the territory and the neighboring countries, will be paramount. But territory, as an indispensable link, remains constant and essential. It is so for reasons of security—political and military—and a military man like Vauban was especially aware of these, but also for reasons of economics, and therefore for the happiness and opportunity of the people.

[12] The information Vauban was asking for was encompassed in the famous French staff map on the scale of 1:80,000, the *Carte d'État-Major,* which covered the whole country and was published from 1818 to 1878. The first edition of the French National Atlas was completed in 1940 under the editorship of Emmanuel de Martonne.

Vauban was not alone in realizing the significance of territory in his time, although he expressed it more convincingly and powerfully than any other author of the period. He was far in advance of his contemporaries in his doctrine and his analysis, and the royal refusal to accept his fiscal project was his greatest defeat. But the role of territory in national policy was gradually being accepted, owing to the need of regulating the distribution of new industries and the construction of new means of transport (canals, roads, seaports) in the various countries.

Regional Inequality and the Need for Regulation

The rapid economic expansion of the sixteenth century caused many shifts and imbalances in western Europe. Despite the wars, religious or dynastic, afflicting most countries with little respite, the seventeenth century saw considerable changes in the structure of society and in the geographical distribution of population and wealth. Both these categories of changes called for political and theoretical debate.

Competition between regions within the national territory was discussed in very lively fashion in France and England during the seventeenth century. In 1615 Antoine de Montchrétien published his *Traicté de l'œconomie,* one of the major manifestoes of mercantilism. The author, following Jean Bodin but in much more technical manner, argues in favor of international trade to develop the national and regional economies. He is still influenced by some medieval regionalism and wishes to avoid inequalities between the various provinces of the kingdom; he therefore also advocates the development of internal trade, and he is conscious of the need to facilitate the migration of labor and the employment of foreigners in order to secure in every place the desirable kind and quantity of manpower. Montchrétien is also very impressed with the extraordinary economic and political expansion achieved in the Netherlands a few years after it became independent. And he pays due attention to the greater role of maritime transport, much cheaper than land transport for bulky cargo,[13] a fact that becomes a new and lasting law of economics.

Such mercantilist attitudes were not shared by all economic experts of the time. Every country was covered by a dense and com-

[13] Montchrétien, *Traicté de l'œconomie politique* (1615; rpt. Paris: Plon, 1889), especially pp. 53–70. See the analysis by Pierre Dockès, *L'espace dans la pensée économique du XVIe au XVIIIe siècle* (Paris, 1969), pp. 99–123.

plicated web of tolls, privileges, and regulations, largely inherited from a feudal past, which made trade difficult and movement of goods costly, especially inland. While pioneers of expansion in government, such as Vauban, wished for a great simplification and standardization of the system, allowing more freedom, the preservation of the old order had its advocates. About 1700, Pierre de Boisguillebert, in a series of pamphlets, took a very nationalistic line, approving of foreign trade mainly to the extent that it benefits the country by limiting benefits to others. He was, however, opposed to the excessive taxes and to all the local and regional shackles imposed inside the kingdom. The need began to emerge for a more unified national market, as wide as possible.

The desirability of foreign trade was argued in England by several important mercantilists, especially Sir Thomas Mun, Sir Josiah Child, and Sir William Temple.[14] The first two were businessmen and directors of the East India Company; Temple was a diplomat and politician. All three were islanders looking outward, very much interested in overseas commerce and very much impressed with the achievements of the Dutch.

More clearly than the French writers of the period, they recognized the competitive situation arising over the seas and in general trade between England and the Netherlands. The seventeenth century was, of course, the great period of English colonization, first in Virginia and Massachusetts, later in the New Netherlands annexed in the 1660s and renamed New York and New Jersey. The Dutch, however, had been extremely successful in taking over a large part of the Portuguese possessions around Africa and in the East Indies. Soon the main rivalry for overseas lands and trade was with France. But the most spectacular expansion due to maritime trade in the seventeenth century was that of the Netherlands, and it also brought to the Dutch an economic and cultural development that made Holland in that "Golden Century" the envy of the world. The English mercantilists saw in foreign trade and sea navigation the indispensable framework for success in the worldwide competition for new territories and for economic progress at home. Since the sixteenth century, England had renewed her claims, put forward also in medieval times, to the "English sovereignty over the British seas." This sovereignty was once more affirmed by Crom-

---

14 See especially Thomas Mun, *A Discourse of Trade from England into the East-Indies* (London, 1621), and *England's Treasure by Forraign Trade* (London, 1664); Sir Josiah Child, *A New Discourse on Trade* (London, 1669); Sir William Temple, *The Works of . . .*, 2 vols. (London, 1720), and several other editions. See also Pierre Dockès, *L'espace*, pp. 124–31.

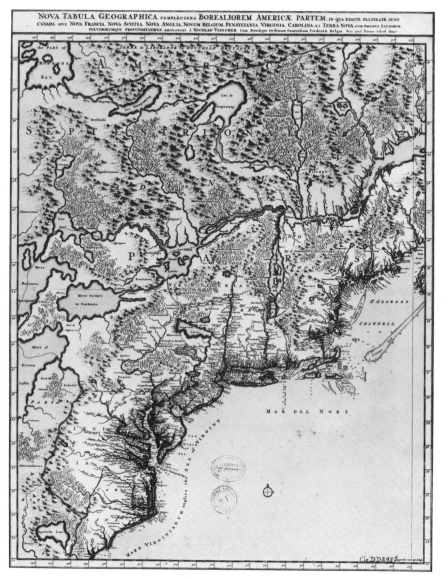

5 A Seventeenth-Century Map of North America. Drawn by the Dutch
cartographer Nicholas Visscher, circa 1670. Courtesy Bibliothèque Nationale,
Paris. Photo S.P.B.N.

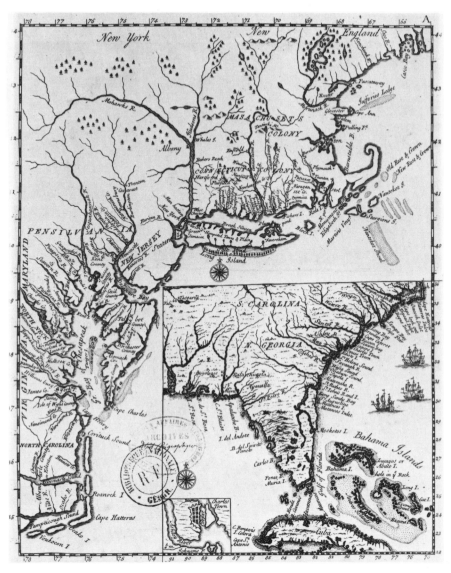

6   A Late Seventeenth-Century Map of the English Colonies in North America. Compare with Visscher's more general map 5. Courtesy Bibliothèque
Nationale, Paris. Photo S.P.B.N.

well's Navigation Acts and acknowledged by the Netherlands in the Treaty of Westminster (1674). Foreign imports began to influence the English way of life, as tea and coffee came on the market in London and in Oxford, where the first coffee-house opened in 1650. Customs regulations became one of the major instruments of the crown to influence the country's economic life.

Official interest in geographical knowledge was spreading fast in Europe. Cartographers were patronized by royalty. Bernhard Varenius, a German scholar, published in 1650 his *Geografia generalis,* a first attempt to outline the general laws of the geography of physical phenomena, demonstrating the great advances of knowledge in this field since Jean Bodin. Generalization about the distribution of population and its various characteristics was still too dangerous a matter to tackle under royal and ecclesiastical censorship, but data-gathering started, and the diffusion of such knowledge proceeded fast. Richard Hakluyt taught geography at the University of Oxford, where Cromwell appointed Sir William Petty as professor of anatomy (1650). This latter title may sound misleading: Petty, by his interests and his writings, was rather a geographer and economist. One of his major contributions, however, was to analyze demographic trends by assessing the mortality and natality in a given area; such research was at that time easily linked to medicine and anatomy.

William Petty was an important writer on matters of territorial organization, much in advance of his time. His interests in population distribution and growth and in surveys are in many respects similar to Vauban's.[15] Petty's writings on Ireland form a valuable geographical treatise on that island, though they also plead for certain reforms. Like Vauban's *Royal Tythe,* Petty's *Political Anatomy of Ireland* (1672) suggests a set of policies based on as careful a survey of conditions in that territory as was then possible.

Still more important are Petty's *Essays on Political Arithmetick* (published between 1676 and 1687) in which he attempted a comparative study of the population, resources, and potential strength of England, France, and Holland.[16] Petty attached special importance to the size of the major cities, compared London with Paris, Rome, and Amsterdam, and argued that the English capital was in

15 It would be interesting to know whether Vauban had read Petty's writings. Both men may have used the common lore of knowledge of their time.

16 There were several editions of Petty's works in the seventeenth and eighteenth centuries. They were gathered and well edited by C. H. Hull as *The Economic Writings of Sir William Petty* (1899; rpt. New York: Augustus M. Kelley, 1963).

the 1680s the largest of all. He also estimated the growth of London through the increasing concentration in the capital of a large part of England's total population, forecasting that, if trends continued as projected, the population of London would absorb all of England's people by 1842.[17]

Petty understood that, despite size in area and population, a country may have potential resources equal to those of bigger and, at a given moment, stronger states. He also appreciated the real importance of such factors as the skills of manpower and the development of maritime activities and of large cities. He is one of the few authors of the time who preferred the concentration of population and economic activity in a very large urban center to an equal spread of people and wealth throughout the whole territory. He seemed to have understood the potential for industrial growth inherent in areas of dense population, an opinion also advanced by Sir William Temple, and probably inspired by the thick settlement of Holland.[18]

The national consciousness developed in that time made scholars realize that, in the competition for power and progress, people were certainly the major factor, both in quantity and quality, but that the use and organization of their territory was the next factor in importance, and one that national policy could not afford to ignore.

By the end of that century it became established usage to survey the population and economic geography of a territory before any new policies or rules for its government were decided, and to compare the observations of the survey with similar data, insofar as available, from other areas of the same kind. A sort of international ethics was being ironed out in western Europe, involving the scientific and scholarly consideration of the right of every state to compete on a free and equal basis for economic opportunity. To defend the position of his country in the international competition against either the established dominance or the aggressive advances of others, every sovereign power endeavored to establish a system of rules fostering its own interests. Some of these rules were formulated in the field of international law, such as the freedom of navigation on the high seas as expounded by Grotius, and others for the internal administration of kingdoms and colonial empires.

---

[17] Petty, *Economic Writings*, II, 464–65 in Kelley's edition.

[18] Petty and Temple sat on the same Committee of the Commons on the means of advancing the trade of Ireland and must have also discussed general economic theory.

A Place in the Sun

It must be remembered that the territories being settled and developed overseas were in the seventeenth century already vying for the attention of central authority and competing for means of achieving greater economic development. The competition started at the home base, in Europe: the various companies set up for trading with the East or West Indies asked for protection and help in their homeland and engaged in active publicity to gain financial and political support.

The Virginia Company, for instance, benefited by the writings and teaching of Richard Hakluyt and of John Smith and, after setbacks in 1622, engaged "no less a person than Dr. John Donne, the poet and dean of St. Paul's, to preach and publish a sermon declaring, somewhat metaphysically, that support of the colony would advance both England and the Kingdom of God."[19] Donne was rewarded with stock in the company. Shortly after 1700 growing pains caused an investigation of conditions in Virginia by commissioners appointed from London, and their report emphasized the distribution of settlement and the characteristics of the Virginia population, comparing it with those of other English colonies in America, especially in New England.[20] The commissioners set forth a program of reforms and recommended the creation of a college to improve the level of education. The College of William and Mary was founded in response.

While private interests, as well as governments in their wake, were actively pursuing the appropriation of new lands wherever they could reach, economic and political doctrine was acknowledging that wealth and power did not come with the simple control of territory. They could be achieved only through an adequate organization and servicing of the acquired portion of space. Such organization required an investment of labor and skill that could not be obtained from the inhabitants of a new territory (the North American Indians were proving especially disappointing to Europeans in this respect). Organization also required maintenance, which could be costly, and military protection from the enterprises

[19] Louis B. Wright, Introduction to *Newes from the New-World*, ed. Louis B. Wright (San Marino, Calif., 1946), p. 5.

[20] Henry Hartwell, James Blair, and Edward Chilton, *The Present State of Virginia and the College* (London, 1727), ed. Hunter D. Farish (Charlottesville, Va., Dominion Books, 1964). See also Jean Gottmann, *Virginia in Our Century* (Charlottesville, Va., 1969), ch. 2.

of adventurous competitors, as the Spaniards and Portuguese early discovered.

The emphasis, in what may appear as a huge set of territory-grabbing operations, was curiously on people and organization. It was, however, taken for granted that to apply their skills and creative potential, people needed space, and that any acquisition of territory, even before actual reconnaissance and settlement, brought about a new potential for putting resources to work.

In Europe itself, the financial profits from economic expansion caused the formation of a whole new stratum of the middle class, people who bought land to ascertain social status and as a secure long-range investment. The landed gentry multiplied rapidly in the seventeenth and eighteenth centuries in France, Germany, and the Netherlands. In the period of the Civil War in England much land changed hands: "The new men of the Tudor period had 'gone into land'; younger sons of landowning families had 'gone into business.' . . . In 1640 more than half of the peerage was subsequent in creation to 1603; many of these new peers were country gentry who had enriched themselves in business undertakings."[21]

There was much social fluidity, despite wars and periods of hard deprivation. There was also talk that "happiness" for the common people ought to be secured by the sovereign for his subjects, and if local conditions, especially religious legislation, were not favorable, people would move elsewhere. The rapidly widening accessible world seemed to offer the possibility of "a place in the sun" for everyone. From England, the Puritans went to Massachusetts, the Quakers to Pennsylvania, the Catholics to Maryland. From France, Protestants migrated to England, Holland, the favorable German states, or even to the English colonies in America. From Massachusetts, dissenters removed to Rhode Island.

This increasing partitioning of an already diversified world was not to the taste of all contemporaries. Blaise Pascal, the French mathematician and philosopher, may well have originated the expression "a place in the sun," in his *Pensées:* "Mine, thine. —This dog is mine, said those poor children; here is my place in the sun.— There is the beginning and the image of the usurpation of the whole globe."[22] Pascal protests against the irrationality of situations

---

[21] E. L. Woodward, *History of England* (London, 1965), pp. 113–14.

[22] Pascal, *Pensées* (édition de Port-Royal, 1670), pt. 1, ch. 2, 9 (my own translation from the reprint in the *Collection de la Pleiade*). See also Gilbert Chinard, *En lisant Pascal* (Geneva, 1948), explaining that in seventeenth-century French *usurpation* did not convey the strong meaning of today and could have meant "to make use" or "lay out."

where a river separates two legal systems making what is right on one side wrong on the other and where truth varies according to which side of a mountain range one lives on.

The mathematical physicist, who contributed much to his age's understanding of the physical universe, believed in the universal truth of principles elaborated by man's reason. He refused to admit the diversifying virtue of space: "It is not from space that I must draw my dignity, but from the regulation of my thought. I shall not have more by possessing lands. Through space, the universe encompasses me and swallows me like a dot; through thought, I can encompass it."[23] The two quoted thoughts must be put together. In Pascal's reasoning, the scientist wants to see only ambition and greed in the subdivision of space by men; the Christian philosopher (and devout Catholic moralist) rebels against the political divisions that assign to every faith and sect the freedom of its own territory. In some way, Pascal probably expressed the opinion of a vast "silent majority" of his time: otherwise the religious wars would not have been so bitter, forcing the territorial separations recognized in the Treaties of Westphalia for Europe, and in the setting up of the numerous English colonies in North America. Metaphysics and scientific method concurred in Pascal's mind to promote principles of universal value.

As a "place in the sun," territory meant a certain freedom from constraints by the world at large, a guarantee of the autonomy of the community's way of life. It did not necessarily guarantee freedom of behavior for the individual. The laws of Massachusetts forbade individual settlement. To settle outside existing towns, at least four families had to get together: such a group could start a separate settlement only by promising to maintain a parson who could also be a teacher. Thus the fulfillment of religious and educational needs could be assured in the new village. Many colonists early disobeyed this rule, and dispersed settlement by isolated families was observed and bemoaned in the seventeenth and even more in the eighteenth century. What the abundance of free land made possible in the New World could not develop in the much more fully occupied countries of Europe, and some kind of territorial division had to be recognized by politics to compensate for the lack of toleration. Territorial jurisdiction, granted to a community that in another geographical frame would be a minority group, provided the means of preserving the group's identity and dignity. Pascal's sentences indicate that he saw these facts but resented them; he would have preferred toleration and, even better, the

23 Pascal, *Pensées*, pt. 1, ch. 3, 1 (my own translation).

recognition by all men of the same, true faith. In paradoxical fashion his thought points out that distinct "places in the sun" were needed because of the lack of fraternity among people, because of human nature, at least in his era. His reasoning also announces the forthcoming trend of thought that transferred the universal generalizations of scientific method to the study of social and political matters.

Recognizing the Diversity and the Unity of Society

The eighteenth century started in most European countries as a period of consolidation of establishment structures, and it ended, having been an era of "enlightenment" in a period of progress, reform, liberalization, and the emergence of nationalism as a popular movement. The economic expansion of the preceding centuries went on. More new space was added as exploration and settlement proceeded inland on the continents, and Australia was discovered in the South Seas. The gradually developing common lore of scientific and technological knowledge produced in the second half of the century the Industrial Revolution, which began in England and soon encompassed the whole northwest of Europe and the northeast of the United States. In this momentous century a double movement of liberalization affected the way in which men looked at the way they were organizing space. Firstly, they recognized the great diversity of societies around the world and within their own countries. Secondly, they came to draw conclusions from the essential role of human labor and skill in the production of wealth. A rapid evolution ensued which, in simplified terms, led to the acceptance of a doctrine claiming that the individual and the constituted community both needed, each in its own way and on its own scale, as much freedom of action as possible to develop resources and achieve happiness. Freedom was also sought in terms of thought, of a liberation from the existing systems of belief, whether religious or political.

The challenges thus emerging to the old and solid structures inherited from the past took many forms. In economics, the eighteenth century saw the rapid growth of the money economy and the use of credit, accompanied by the appearance of paper bank notes as a major means of financial settlement; it also saw much expansion in a variety of securities and the recognition of stock exchanges as established institutions. The first instruments of large-scale credit management appeared in London in the 1690s with the Bank of

England and the office of marine insurance at Lloyd's coffee house.

Resources became increasingly abstract and subject to speculative ventures. There was a fading away of the old stability of basic wealth founded on the land itself, that is, either on the products of the land or on the control of strategic points passed by overland transportation. It would seem that the concept of territory ought to have vanished from the doctrinal debate as well as from the concerns of politics. In fact, the contrary happened: few other periods in history were so territory-conscious. The modern concept of territorial sovereignty as exclusive national jurisdiction emerged, as we have known it since, at the end of the eighteenth century.

The concern for human diversification in space took various forms. In the first third of the century it was expressed in satirical writings by learned authors: Jonathan Swift published *Gulliver's Travels* in 1726 in London and Montesquieu's *Lettres persanes* was anonymously published in Paris in 1721. Both books had an immediate and enormous success. Using different stratagems, the authors described a variety of countries coexisting in the same world, though ignoring or despising one another; each country has its own culture, which pretends to be the best and highest of all, and each insists on being completely different from the others. The description of strange people or creatures leads easily to satire of the author's own society, in a manner that censorship could hardly condemn. *Gulliver's Travels* has remained to this time a great classic in European education; several of the strange words coined by Swift, such as *Lilliputians,* have become common nouns in many languages. With his light style and exuberant fantasy, telling about giants, Lilliputians, flying islands, and Yahoos, Gulliver is a delight for children and adults and may be considered the perfect introduction to an understanding of internationalism.

Montesquieu's book is for sophisticated adults. The correspondence of a Persian nobleman visiting France, with his friends and wives at home, not only illustrates the differences between two distant cultures with different religions and legal systems, it also insists on the variety of the Europeans themselves, as the Persian reports with sarcasm the astonishment of a French friend at the behavior of some Spaniards and the amazement of the latter at some gestures of the Portuguese. Montesquieu stresses the differences between the nations, but also hints at all the common features of human nature and of social and political organization. In many ways *Lettres persanes* is an ancestor of social anthropology, and also of what has recently developed as a "perceptionist" approach to human geography.

But Montesquieu is most interested in the diversity of the legal systems in the world and the relationships that may be observed between a system of laws and the various characteristics, physical, human, and political, of the country where it is applied. His fundamental work, *The Spirit of Laws,* appeared in 1748, summing up a lifetime of scholarship and opening new vistas to social studies.[24]

Montesquieu was seeking principles of universal value in the causes and effects of laws. In a time when churchmen still controlled education and scholarly research, his major endeavor was to demonstrate that the social and political life of the various peoples on earth does not result from metaphysical causes but from the combined effects of many factors that can be traced and analyzed, some resulting from local, natural conditions and some from what he calls "moral causes." The latter are products of history, economics, and legislation.

The Spirit of Laws encompasses all the knowledge the author had gathered, in his reading and his travels, on the various legal systems past and present. It attempts to show the causes and effects of legislation. Often what is only reporting of an opinion found to have been expressed about some matter has been mistakenly treated as a conclusion. A vast treatise, the work encompasses so much data that almost every statesman could have found in it points to adopt or to criticize. The empress of Russia, Catherine the Great, was reported to have been delighted by a sentence stating that the sovereign of a very large empire needed unlimited power. Laws are examined in relation to military matters, the freedom of the citizen, systems of taxation, types of climate and of "terrain," national customs, commerce and money, demography, religion, and so forth.

Nineteenth-century analysts labelled Montesquieu a "physical determinist" because of the considerable space he allocated to such natural causes as climate and terrain. More careful recent studies have shown this opinion to be erroneous. Montesquieu insists more, in fact, on the effect of the "moral" causes. Natural causes, he felt, are dominant only with primitive people. More advanced civilizations have liberated themselves from the impact of natural conditions. Moreover, as Robert Shackleton has shown, in the French language of that time *climat* meant the sum total of the geographical features of a territory, including location. Similarly, *terrain* was

24 Charles-Louis de Secondat, Baron de Montesquieu, *De l'esprit des lois* (Geneva, 1748). Montesquieu (1689–1755) spent the last years of his life defending his book against criticism by the Catholic Church. See biographical data accompanying the Preface by Roger Caillois to Montesquieu, *Oeuvres complètes,* Bibliothèque de la Pléiade (Paris, 1951), I, xxvi.

used in a wider sense than its modern topographic meaning: it included soils and land use.[25]

There is no doubt today that civilized societies do not behave according to the dictates of the environing natural conditions but use the conditions for their own purposes, which differ with time and place. It nevertheless remains important to stress that these natural conditions are factors to be reckoned with. This was a rather new approach for the political and juridical thought of the eighteenth century, and one of Montesquieu's important contributions was to bring it into the analysis of human societies. Earlier writers, especially classical authors such as Hippocrates and Herodotus, had hinted at such relationships, and Jean Bodin's influence was also to be accounted for, but like every author, Montesquieu used the accumulated lore of his time.[26] Although his doctrine may have been misunderstood or diversely interpreted, his method changed the way people looked at their own structures; it established a new vogue of relating the geographical characteristics of a territory to its politics.

It is significant that, two years after *The Spirit of Laws* was published, a young and brilliant graduate of the Sorbonne attempted to outline a new discipline, which he called "political geography." Upon his graduation in 1750, Turgot delivered two remarkable addresses on the progress of mankind, and he then began his attempt to develop a political geography.[27] It was an ambitious scheme, aiming at a full tableau of "theoretical" and "positive" relationships between the facts of geography, understood as all facts, physical and human, of spatial distribution, and the political process. Young Turgot (then twenty-three) was obsessed with the ideals of geographical order and of historical progress, which he wanted government to understand and reconcile. He was obviously under the spell of Vauban's and Montesquieu's works, but far too much in advance of the practical politics of his time. His career in government and his economic writings emphasized the need to base policies on solid geographical knowledge and to liberate workers

[25] The best recent analysis of Montesquieu's doctrine is in Shackleton's *Montesquieu: A Critical Biography* (Oxford, 1961), especially ch. 11–14.

[26] Both Swift and Montesquieu had read and annotated Bodin's writings. The latter had Bodin's works in his library at the Chateau de La Brède, and the Yale University Library owns a copy of Bodin's *De la république* annotated by Swift. Shackleton, *op. cit.*, has also shown the influence on Montesquieu of the little-known works of Espiard.

[27] See "Géographie politique," in *Oeuvres de Turgot*, ed. Eugene Daire (Paris, 1844), II, 611–26. This edition includes the footnotes by Dupont de Nemours.

from all the servitudes imposed on the common people by the laws of the time.

It is also significant that exactly one hundred years after Varenius published in his *General Geography* the first treatise on the general physical features of the globe, Turgot attempted a "political geography" which would have brought human behavior and the political process into a general theory related to physical phenomena. The progress is striking of ideas endeavoring to understand the partitioning and organization of inhabited space in the light of the interplay between natural conditions and human activity. Emphasis on the variety of the world leads to an analysis in which some territorial units are recognized as meaningful elements, culturally and politically.

At the same time, recognition of the diversity of societies and of the similarity of each of them led to comparative and competitive examination. The great eighteenth-century political writers concurred in wishing for more freedom for individuals to develop and pursue their own interests. Such pursuit they believed to be beneficial to the community as a whole. Montesquieu felt that there was no climate in which people who enjoyed enough freedom could not be made to work productively, but that men might be accused of being "lazy" where freedom was lacking and laws improperly made. A great doctrine was emerging, recommending freedom for all men in a world where serfdom, indenture, and slavery had long been common. At the same time it was advanced that every nation should be allowed to elaborate its own system of laws. Europe was evolving from a unified and pyramidal order toward plurality and the fluidity of greater freedom.

Empires and Revolutions

Such was the intellectual trend, but it conflicted with legislation in most monarchies, where absolutism was still dominant, and with the imperial policies of the governments that had built colonial systems overseas. Easily conquering vast new continents, European powers found that opposition came usually, even overseas, from one of their European neighbors. Control of large territories and populations overseas changed hands by treaties signed in Europe, between Europeans, after wars largely decided by battles on the continent or on the high seas. Many countries passed from one empire to another by such agreements: in 1713 by the Peace of Utrecht, Spain ceded some South American lands to Portugal, and France ceded Newfoundland and Hudson Bay to England; in 1763 by the Peace of Paris French possessions in Canada and India and several Spanish islands in the West Indies were ceded to England. To the east of Europe, the Russian Empire was rapidly expanding at the expense of Sweden on the Baltic, of Turkey around the Black Sea, of China on the Amur River. Peter the Great and Catherine II had opened Russia to the trade and the cultural influences of the West. Russia agreed with Prussia and Austria to divide Poland between the three powers. It seemed that only great European empires counted as active factors in world politics.

Suddenly the Boston Tea Party in 1773, followed by the American Declaration of Independence in 1776, challenged the structure and unity of the British Empire, the most rapidly and successfully expanding of all. The American Revolution involved demands for equality in the opportunities of overseas trade and of liberty in terms of self-government. The story is too well known to need much reporting here. It was the first major move toward the gradual breaking up of the overseas colonial empires formed around the world by the western European powers, a process still unfinished.

The essence of the American Revolution for the purposes of this analysis was in the demand for independent self-government by a group of colonies located on distant shores but belonging predominantly to the same national stock and culture as the peoples of the United Kingdom. The fact that they inhabited a different part of the world had given to these Americans the feeling of being a fairly distinct community. The conflict developed as a result of taxation imposed by central authority from London, and the famous cry of "No taxation without representation" arose in response. Also, London wanted to maintain for the British companies monopolistic rights to the intercontinental maritime trade, a major source of revenue: hence, the Boston Tea Party.

The empire at that time largely appeared as a huge maritime system. The faraway territories could be a source of revenue for the central government only by the trade they supplied and the taxes they paid. It was costly to maintain troops in so many territories to assure their security as well as a navy to control the sea lanes. The peace of 1763 had concluded a long and costly war, and the Royal Treasury needed to expand the flow of income. The American colonists felt they were being exploited. They wanted to participate in the running of their own affairs and in the opportunities opened up on the sea by imperial expansion and on their own continent by the acquisition from France in 1763 of western territories extending to the Mississippi. The London government naturally felt that the authority to dispose of the western lands as well as the general direction of imperial maritime trade should remain in its hands.

There were indeed several causes of tension. A major point was that the population of the colonies by 1770 had reached 2.2 million people, the size of a nation by eighteenth-century standards. Most of the colonists were American-born. Large cities had grown at the major seaports and had engaged in overseas trade. By 1775 Philadelphia was probably the second or third largest city in the empire. Now that British ships dominated the high seas and the French had definitely lost control of North America, the Americans felt they could take care of their own security. Thus the cry of "liberty" arose and the Revolution started.

The Declaration of Independence had been preceded by statements by James Wilson and Thomas Jefferson to the effect that 'all the different members of the British Empire are distinct States, independent of each other.' A certain allegiance to the crown, still accepted in 1774 when Wilson and Jefferson seemed amenable to a political structure like that of the modern British Commonwealth, was rejected in 1776. The Declaration, drafted under Jefferson's leadership, affirmed the right "of the people to . . . institute new government, laying its foundation on such principles and organizing its powers in such form, as to them shall seem most likely to effect their safety and happiness."

Thus security and opportunity were to be reconciled, and both were to be provided by national sovereignty over the inhabited territory. An exclusive jurisdiction was claimed in the name of the *nation*, that is, the collective body politic of the population. The medieval inheritance of government by divine right or by virtue of allegiance to the person of the sovereign was liquidated in America by the independence of the United States. The Treaty of Paris of 1783 formally acknowledged recognition by the United Kingdom and France. The American Constitution set up a democratic form of government, a federal structure with some decentralization of powers, and a unified national market for the movement of goods and people. Finally, the principles of the separation of church and state and of general religious tolerance were inserted into the Constitution by the first amendments (the Bill of Rights), which came into force in 1791.

By that date another revolution had shattered another large political structure: the French Revolution, begun in July 1789, established a definite and decisive link between territorial sovereignty and the national population. Because this happened in a

European country that controlled one of the largest colonial empires, the effect was soon felt in several parts of the world. In France the revolutionary assemblies and governments stressed national sovereignty and national unity. The intricate system of tolls, fees, and internal customs was simplified and a unified market established over the whole national territory. Territorial unity and integrity were stressed by the formula of "La République, une et indivisible," which applied in the political as well as the economic spheres.

The political reforms went much further by proposing a new philosophy for the rights and ethics of the individual citizen, who was to live by the trilogy "Liberty, Equality, and Fraternity." To defend the new regime and the Republic's sacred soil the nation was called to arms, and conscription was established, to remain in France, creating a large army made up of the whole physically fit citizenry. The formula *pro patria mori* became official policy, written into law. Refusing consideration of any federal system, creating a new, standardized, centralized, and strongly hierarchical domestic administration, cancelling all the privileges of Church and nobility, the French Revolution drew the plans for a monolithic national state. Her policies revived and clarified the claims, heard since Richelieu, to the "natural frontiers" of France. The territorial base of the political structure seemed very important to the idealistic and utopian statesmen. A strong element of ideological intolerance, however, was built into this revolutionary process, a situation that Jefferson early understood and worried about, as his letters from Paris show.

The American and French revolutions opened a new era, in which national states are based on clear-cut territorial sovereignty exercised by the government solely in the name of the nation. This pattern was to be generally adopted and was to lay at the foundation of the political partitioning of the world two hundred years later. Gradually the dynastic and imperial principles were to fade out of the tableau, and the rights of the people to self-government in the territory they inhabited were to be increasingly recognized. Religious differences, however, and geographical contiguity continued to play an essential part in territorial claims. Religion remained a strong binding force in human communities; religious strife remained a cause of political tension in many parts of the world, and statesmen often sought to solve such problems by territorial division and separation. The doctrine of contiguity as a source of rights or privileges in neighboring territory has been systematically frowned upon by international law, but in political practice many conflicts and territorial changes resulted from debates between contiguous powers, some feeling threatened by neighbors, others feeling that their citizens' rights to the opportunities available next to their borders were unjustly denied.

The national states that emerged from the two great revolutions at the end of the eighteenth century were, in fact, very dissimilar. The United States was pluralistic, needing territorial expansion on its continent, immigration from overseas, and large-scale maritime trade. Within its immediate area the country felt secure, except during the brief episode of the War of 1812 with Great Britain. The first French Republic was indeed monistic in its political philosophy and structure. It was mainly concerned with self-defense and with advancing the individual rights of its citizenry, but a strong missionary spirit produced a dynamism that could hardly escape involvement in international conflict.

When Napoleon Bonaparte took control of the French government, he also took immediate advantage of the French dynamism to carry out ambitious policies. The Napoleonic Empire was spectacular though brief. It revived old dynastic practices, bringing the pope to Paris for Napoleon's coronation and later appointing members of Napoleon's family and staff as kings of various European countries.

National States and International Systems

The evolution toward the new system of independent national states was slow but steady. The models set by the independence of the United States and by the first French Republic were followed in different parts of the world. As may have been expected, other notable and successful revolutions proclaiming the independence of former colonies were to develop first in the Americas. In Haiti the large population of slaves brought from Africa had obtained their liberation by an edict of the French Revolution, but the ensuing tensions with the French landowners led to a revolution and the proclamation of independence from France in 1804. Napoleon, after the defeat of his fleet at Trafalgar and the collapse of the regime he had temporarily installed in Egypt (1798–1801) was well aware of his weakness on the seas. His ambitions turned to the continent of Europe and he preferred to sell to the United States in 1803 the French rights to Louisiana.

The next revolution swept a whole continent: the Spanish colonies in America claimed their independence, refusing from 1810 to recognize Joseph Bonaparte as king of Spain. The restoration of the Bourbon dynasty in Madrid was answered by the Declaration of Independence of the United Provinces of the Rio de la Plata in 1816, followed by the foundation of the republics of Argentina (1816), Chile (1818), Colombia (1819), Peru (1821), Santo Domingo, and so forth. In 1822, Brazil declared its independence of Portugal, becoming, like Mexico, an "empire" in her own right. Most of South and Central America became independent and was subdivided into a number of separate national states.

In the same period the political geography of the European continent was reshaped in several ways. Napoleon had built a vast empire, of which the various countries remained, however, officially distinct states. He believed in the virtue of a certain clearcut territorial order which he labored to design. To show respect for the principle of national sovereignty affirmed by the French Revolution he called himself "emperor of the French" and not of "France." He took the titles of Mediator of the Swiss Confederation and Protector of the German Federation of the Rhineland. However, he also styled himself king of Italy. In Germany and Italy he worked at simplifying the political map, absorbing some of the smaller states left over by the medieval past into larger units of government. He advanced considerably the trend toward unification of these two countries. Similarly, he insisted (and stipulated in peace treaties) that the Hapsburg emperor reigning in Vienna give up the title of Holy Roman German Emperor (thus liquidating the diplomatic remnants of the Holy Roman Empire) and become just emperor of Austria.[28] The door was open for the unification of Germany in 1871 as an empire separate from that of Austria-Hungary.

The organization of the German space in the middle of Europe had caused various discussions in political theory since the Peace of Westphalia in 1648 had granted territorial sovereignty to all the German states. In the eighteenth century the philosophy of Kant was brought into the debate. Johann Gottlieb Fichte, inspired by the rights of nations as recognized by the American and French constitutions, was propagating ideas of the natural rights of a nation to the territory around it.[29] The French revolutionary armies sweeping through Germany and Italy were bringing with them

[28] In the short-lived Peace of Amiens with Great Britain (1802), Napoleon insisted that English sovereigns give up the meaningless title of king of France used in British documents since the claims of the fourteenth century.

[29] Fichte advocated government-controlled national economies in *The Isolated Commercial State* (1800).

ideals not only of democracy, liberty, and equality, but also of national unity and identity, which had not been previously popularized in those countries. The possibility arose of a "new European ideology," compatible with the coexistence within Europe of national states. The Germans had lived under the vague, general framework of the Holy Roman Empire, which was composed of national states often disputing among themselves. In the eighteenth century the Swedish predominance crumbled, Prussia expanded, some Polish provinces were added, and a rising pressure from Russia was felt in the east.

In 1797 Novalis published a pamphlet entitled *Christenheit oder Europa*. Indeed the unity of Europe as the Christian continent was crumbling in more obvious fashion than ever since the upper Middle Ages, and a political writer wondered whether a geographical entity called Europe could succeed it or a universal concept of Christendom would arise. While the French offered a new, rather radical political philosophy, the monarchs of Europe formed a coalition against the French to keep the "revolutionary hydra" away from their peoples. Napoleon certainly hoped to be able to build European unity on another basis, incorporating some of the phraseology and reforms of the revolution within a political structure traditional enough to reassure the conservative elements. He established an "empire" different from the Holy Roman Empire that he abolished; he insisted on associating the pope and the Church with his rule, but he applied policies of religious toleration and gave official status to several religions, including the Jewish, in the countries he governed.

When he realized, after 1805, that England could not be defeated while the British maritime supremacy could isolate Europe, Napoleon tried to cut England off from Europe: the Continental System was inaugurated with the Berlin Decree (1806), but led to a final break and war with Russia, as Czar Alexander I refused to abide by the system (1812). Napoleon was defeated by the allied forces of Europe in 1814, and a new map of the continent was drawn at the Congress of Vienna (1814–15). Most of the European countries joined in a Holy Alliance to protect peace and order, and to oppose revolutionary movements, under the leadership of Russia and Austria. It seemed that a new conservative unity was forming for Europe, although England refrained from joining the Holy Alliance and Turkey was kept out.[30]

Peace in Europe and the restoration of royal dynasties unseated

[30] See Felix Markham, *Napoleon and the Awakening of Europe* (London, 1950).

by the French Revolution and Napoleon accelerated, however, the revolutionary trend in the Spanish colonies in America. By 1822 independence had been proclaimed from Mexico to Chile, but these new republics and empires seemed fragile and unstable, and the situation was viewed with some alarm in Washington. This apprehension was understandable; the major wounds of the wars of the French Revolution and Empire having healed after a few years of peace and reorganization, Europe looked rather united and recovered. There was some likelihood that the still prosperous and dynamic continent, reinforced by the active participation of the vast power of Russia, would choose to apply its energies overseas. France had lost almost all her colonies, mainly to England, from 1763 to 1815, and may have wished to succeed Spain in some parts of America. Russia had been expanding on the seas: in 1821 Alexander I issued a ukase claiming as territory of New Russia the northwest seaboard of North America from the Bering Strait to 51 ° north latitude, that is, to Vancouver Island. Russia also claimed the northern parts of the Pacific Ocean between that coast and the Siberian shores. In 1821, at the other end of the globe, Fabian von Bellinghausen, sailing under the Russian flag, explored the approaches to the Antarctic icecap. Alexander I spoke as the unchallenged leader of the Holy Alliance.

The American relations with England, though much improved since the war of 1812, were still strained; there were rumors of English designs on Cuba. In these circumstances the message received in 1823 from the British foreign minister, George Canning, proposing a joint Anglo-American declaration to protect the American republics from European intervention, was a welcome surprise. President James Monroe and his secretary of state, John Quincy Adams, decided to act alone, trusting that England would accept and tacitly support a unilateral American declaration. A cautious statesman, Monroe consulted his predecessors Thomas Jefferson and James Madison before deciding. They concurred in approving the doctrine that was set forth in the famous presidential message to Congress of 2 December 1823.

Jefferson's letter to James Monroe, dated 23 October 1823, and giving his opinion of the proposed diplomatic move, has often been quoted as expressing an important tenet of the American creed:

Our first and fundamental maxim should be never to entangle ourselves in the broils of Europe. Our second, never to suffer Europe to intermeddle with cis-Atlantic affairs. America, North and South, has a set of interests distinct from those of Europe, and peculiarly her own. She should, therefore, have a system of her own, separate and apart from that of Europe.[31]

Thus Europe and the Americas are described as two separate political "systems," separated by the Atlantic Ocean. Jefferson's letter would deserve being quoted in full: the elder statesman clearly saw that American security required keeping the European powers from crossing the ocean and that those powers could not afford a

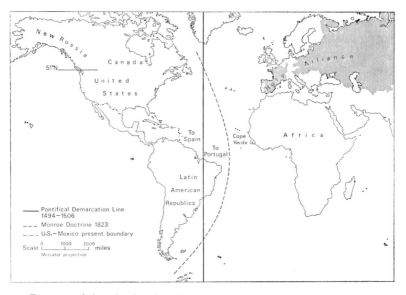

7 Europe and America in 1832. Two separate systems in the era of the Monroe Doctrine.

transoceanic venture against the dominant British sea power. As Sir Charles Webster has put it recently: "the only Power which could challenge it [the Monroe Doctrine] successfully was committed to action which prevented her from doing so."[32]

The Monroe Doctrine, as formulated in 1823, has remained an

[31] The Writings of Thomas Jefferson, ed. P. L. Ford (Washington, D.C., 1899), X, 277–79.

[32] C. K. Webster, Introduction to Britain and the Independence of Latin America, I (London, 1938). See also Samuel F. Bemis, A Diplomatic History of the United States (New York, 1936); Walter Lippman, United States Foreign Policy (New York, 1938); and H. W. V. Temperley, The Foreign Policy of Canning (London, 1940).

important principle in international affairs for a century and a half. It was still invoked in the American opposition to Russian bases in Cuba in 1960–62. It has been a model for the organization of large-scale regional "systems," to use the Jeffersonian term. The American system led to the formation in 1890 of the International Union of the American Republics, later reorganized as the Pan American Union and, after 1948, as the Organization of American States. The concept of the "Western Hemisphere" is another version of the same doctrine, separating the Americas as a distinct system. Several other large-scale systems have recently been formed on a regional scale. In the 1930s Japan organized a short-lived Greater East Asia Co-Prosperity Sphere under its control. After World War II, a group of communist countries in eastern Europe, led by the U.S.S.R., formed the Comecon. In western Europe, the European Economic Community (or Common Market) arose and grew. A League of Arab States was formed in 1945, as former colonies and protectorates in the Middle East achieved independence. In 1963, thirty African countries signed a charter creating an Organization of African Unity.

All these organizations have in common with the Monroe Doctrine a system of distinct common interests due to location in a certain part of the world, a fair degree of contiguity, and a policy endeavoring to prevent interference by powers from other areas. The Monroe Doctrine of 1823 set a model and a trend that is still developing and that has been more imitated in the second half of the twentieth century than in the first hundred years after Monroe.

The geographical regionalization of political systems appears to blossom when a number of national states achieve independence or political recasting and look forward to a new kind of destiny. This coincidence, far from being a paradox, may well be a logical consequence of the consciousness such states achieve of their relative weakness and frailty. The large-scale regional system would have the dual purpose of reinforcing their security and of broadening the framework of economic opportunity. The latter was certainly prevalent among the considerations that led to the formation of the Common Market when western European countries felt smaller and more isolated, especially in relation to the huge size and economic machinery of the contemporary Superpowers. Security was an essential consideration in the organization of the Comecon for countries with a past of political independence, but in which the Communist regimes were fairly new and felt a need of protection by the Soviet Union in their domestic affairs as much as in foreign relations. Although all the multiplying national states achieve freedom of action, they know that this liberty does not make them equal to the more established powers, and they recognize that they are especially unequal in economic and cultural matters.

The Wealth of Nations

The progress of world trade, of the development of distant lands, and of the Industrial Revolution in the eighteenth and nineteenth centuries brought about a shift of emphasis in politics from military and religious matters to economics. This could well have been expected, even in the seventeenth century, from the writings of Vauban, Petty, and Temple (see above, pp. 58–64). It became obvious in the latter part of the eighteenth century. It was not mere coincidence that Thomas Jefferson defined government in the Declaration of Independence as a compact formed to protect "life, liberty and *the pursuit of happiness*" in the same year that Adam Smith published his celebrated *Inquiry into the Nature and Causes of the Wealth of Nations*. The "pursuit of happiness" has been often interpreted, certainly in too restricted fashion, to mean the right to property. That it went much further is evidenced by many statements of that era.[33] But even in the restricted sense, "happiness" was an economic concept, leading politics into a concern for the economic security (not only the physical) of the common man. Indeed most of the targets pursued by the early leaders of the American and French revolutions were economic in nature, though they were to be attained by political and legal means. Those who sought political independence or a democratic form of government were also aiming at *the free control of the resources in their territory*.

Adam Smith summed up in his book most of the economic knowledge of his time, better organized and systematized than it had ever been previously; he spoke of the people in many nations, their organization, their governments. The internal organization was important to him since land use and urban development were recognized as factors of wealth, but essentially he was dealing with political matters, with the effects of laws and policies on economic behavior. He saw every nation as an economic unit on her territory and as the sum total of so many individuals producing and consuming. His book seemed divorced from immediate objectives in

---

[33] Among the latter it may be worthwhile to point to the utterance of the French radical revolutionary Saint-Just: "L'idée de bonheur commence de se répandre de par le monde" (the idea of happiness begins to spread throughout the world).

time and place (although the discussion of the colonies was easy to criticize after 1776) and to be aiming at constant and general relationships: hence his great scientific value and success.

But *The Wealth of Nations* proposed rules for the economic organization of countries, whether independent or not. It was aimed at advising governments how to proceed in the competition among nations for wealth and for progress. Adam Smith expressed the rather optimistic belief of his century in progress, provided liberty was granted to individuals on one hand and to states on the other so that they could reap the fruits of an expanding economy. Wealth was to Smith the product of skill and organization of the nation, "whatever be the soil, climate or extent of territory"; and it was demonstrated by the abundance of the supply of "all the necessaries and conveniences" people desire.[34] The organization of the territory would be, of course, important, but that was just one aspect of the nation's skills. At a time of rapid advances in technology and labor productivity and of the opening up of vast continents to settlement and development, such a frame of mind was quite justified.

As all his biographers have noted, Adam Smith spent several years in France, where he discussed matters with the major economists. Turgot, who had been much interested in the territorial and geographical substratum of the political process, was one of them. At that time, François Quesnay and the physiocrats in Paris were stressing agriculture and therefore the land as the major source of wealth. The cities and industries were, in their view, peripheral developments, a sort of network of satellite phenomena. During this era of enlightenment, European science made great strides; it was the time of Réaumur and Boerhaave, Buffon and Benjamin Franklin, Cavendish and Rutherford, Laplace and Lavoisier. The French Encyclopedists greatly impressed their contemporaries with the power of nature and with an enormous gathering of new data — from which deductions were made often too hastily.

While laying the foundations of modern science in many respects, the eighteenth century made it fashionable to explain the involved and yet little-understood phenomena in the human sciences by physical and natural causes that were supposed to determine them. Even Montesquieu insisted on natural characteristics (climate and terrain) in his discussion of the variety of juridical systems. As America came into the limelight, various naturalists, Buffon and the Abbé Raynal among the more famous, offered a

---

[34] Introduction to Adam Smith, *An Inquiry into the Nature and Causes of the Wealth of Nations* (London, 1776).

theory asserting that the climate and terrain of America restricted physical and biological development. Most of the scholarly opinions, based on spotty and vague reports, concurred in expressing grave doubts that the resources of North America could be developed so as to support a large population of European immigrants.[35] In his *Notes on Virginia,* originally written to give the French better information about his state, Jefferson dwelt at length on the natural features that would refute the assertions of European naturalists, especially Buffon.

The economic theory of the physiocrats, basing the wealth of areas on their agricultural production and natural endowment, was in tune with the scholarly spirit of the time, at least on the continent of Europe.[36] Even Turgot, although recognizing the role of industries and commerce in economic growth, believed that natural conditions and frontiers in the long run determined the size and contours of states. A few other authors, echoing the mercantilism of the seventeenth century, opposed the man-made activities to the natural factors as causes of economic disparity. In France the most important of these after Montesquieu was probably Condillac, who, though originally a naturalist, published an interesting volume on the relationship between commerce and government in 1776.[37] Appearing at the same time as Smith's *Wealth of Nations,* Condillac's work gained little popularity; it was not of the same breadth and depth, but it is interesting for its attempt to visualize a geography of economic activities in an abstract, closed, territorial circuit.

At the end of the century France lost most of her colonies and overseas trade. It was still the most populous state, and the largest in area, in Europe west of Russia. The liberal economics of Adam Smith's school was, of course, known and appreciated in Paris, but the interest was bound to remain centered on the unified but limited internal market of the nation. Napoleon's trends toward European and even regional self-sufficiency, tested during the Continental System policy, and then the relative recoiling after the defeats of 1814–15, made French economic and political thought turn to internal organization and domestic problems. This gave more importance to territory and to the social resources within it. In this same period the German states went through much reorganization

---

[35] See Gilbert Chinard, "Eighteenth Century Theories on America as a Human Habitat," *Proceedings of the American Philosophical Society,* XCI (February 25, 1947), 27–57.

[36] See Georges Weulersse, *Le mouvement physiocratique en France de 1756 à 1770* (Paris, 1910).

[37] Etienne Bonnot de Condillac, *Le commerce et le gouvernement considérés relativement l'un à l'autre* (Paris, 1776).

and redesigning of their internal boundaries; they felt the need to discuss the viability of a European system or of a closed self-sufficient state of less than continental proportions. Novalis and Fichte were expressing in their writings around 1800 a lively debate within the German political and intellectual arena.

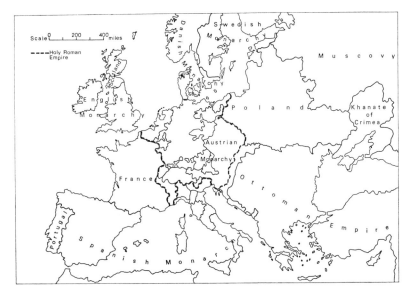

8   Europe in 1815: the Aftermath of Napoleon. *C.H.*, Switzerland.

In England and in the United States circumstances were quite different: the territorial framework looked expanding, worldwide, almost unlimited. The seas were open and free. Early in the nineteenth century, having secured full oceanic supremacy, Great Britain dropped her old claims to the sovereignty of the British seas or to a *mare clausum.* The Dutch doctrine of the freedom of the high seas was adopted beyond the limit of territorial waters, the latter being determined by the range of a cannon shot, as proposed by the Dutch lawyer Bynkershoek in 1737, and recognized to be three miles from the shore.[38] The English-speaking countries, followed

[38] Cornelius van Bynkershoek, "De dominio maris dissertatio" in *Questiones Juris Publici* (Amsterdam, 1737), book I, VIII: "the dominion of the lands ends where the power of the arms ends." See Wyndham L. Walker, "Territorial Waters: The Cannon-Shot Rule," *British Year Book of International Law* (London, 1945), pp. 210–31, and C. John Colombos, *International Law of the Sea,* 6th ed. (London, 1968), pp. 87–99.

to some extent by the Netherlands and Switzerland, were looking toward a more open use of territories and an expansion of free trade. The other countries of Europe were then turning inward.

Structuring the Domestic Economy

The question of whether a national economy ought to be more or less open to the outside world remained a major concern of government and a matter debated in scholarly circles into the twentieth century. The purpose of economic policy is, however, basically internal and domestic, as shown by the origin of the term *economy* (from Greek *oikos,* "house"). Studying the wealth of nations, in governmental terms, has the utility of clarifying how the nation for which that government is responsible could be made wealthy, and therefore secure and happy.

The pursuit of internal happiness in a national state is not hence a matter of satisfying the state as a whole, an anonymous, almost abstract concept. It must aim at the happiness of the population, and the latter may be considered either as individuals (which will involve abstracting them into groupings) or as local communities. The government representing the national body politic is selected either by individual votes or by representatives of communities geographically defined on a local or regional basis. As constitutions grew more democratic, especially in the nineteenth century, individual voters and local communities became more potent factors in politics and legislation.

The local interests often made themselves heard before the advent of democracy. In feudal and absolutist regimes, provinces and cities expressed their claims and interests through various channels, and some sort of attention had to be given to such pressures and utterances. It was only from the seventeenth century on, however, that enough centralized authority was achieved for government agencies to gather data on the economic conditions in the various parts of a country. The diversity of the different provinces then became apparent. The work of Sir William Petty in England and Ireland and that of Marshal de Vauban in France were decisive landmarks. Progress in data gathering and statistical work through the eighteenth century led to the first official systematic censuses of population in the more advanced countries by 1790–1800.

Precise information about the distribution of population within the territory and its gradual changes, especially by migration, became officially available in that period, and governments had to concern themselves with inequalities between regions and with general demographic trends. Economic growth resulting from the expansion of trade and from the first manufactures caused changes in the geographical and occupational distribution of the people. In seventeenth-century England Petty observed a great deal of concentration in London and its environs and forecast a huge urban growth.[39] At the same time the French statesman Jean Baptiste Colbert, establishing royal manufactures in and around Paris, worried about the planning of the French capital. Vauban pointed out the inequalities between the French provinces and stressed the need to help the poorer, more backward sections.

Petty definitely favored the growth of large cities and of the concentration of economic activities other than agriculture in a small number of selected places. The questions of concentration or dispersal of economic activity, and of the resulting employment and wealth, preoccupied many economists in the eighteenth century. Most of them, either liberals or physiocrats, expressed a serious desire for more equality between regions; they preferred to spread industries and wealth equally over the whole territory, if possible. Trends toward concentration worried them, and many authors suggested decentralizing policies.

The Industrial Revolution certainly worked in the direction of greater concentration of population, manufactures, and trade in cities and towns. The competition between local firms and localities largely rested on the availability of a plentiful supply of cheap labor. In an entirely free economy the concentration of population would have proceeded even faster, increasing the inequalities between regions. In the nineteenth century, with the triumph of the steam engine and of coal as the major source of energy, the concentration was accelerated and industries and urbanization gathered and throve in the areas where coal was cheaply mined and in the major seaports.

The eighteenth century, while learning about economic development, new technology, and the wonders of nature, gave a great deal of attention to the internal organization of territory in terms of benefits that could be derived from proper planning by the people and the state. Attempts at a general theory of economic geography can be found in the writings of several of the early economists. Indeed, Vauban, William Petty, and Sir William Temple were pioneers in precisely that field. In 1767 an English economist, Sir James

[39] *Another Essay in Political Arithmetick concerning the Growth of the City of London* (London, 1683) .

Steuart, published a large treatise on "political economy."[40] Like
Condillac's work in France, it appeared too close to the date of the
publication of *The Wealth of Nations* to make a lasting impact. A
number of Steuart's observations show a very good understanding
of his times. His opinions are conservative and strongly antiutopian
and his method rather geographical, often proceeding by case studies from which generalizations are sometimes cautiously deduced.

Steuart is well aware that in the preceding three hundred years
great discoveries, industry and learning, trade and the arts, and the
establishment of public credit and of general taxation have "al-
tered entirely government everywhere." "Formerly, everything was
brought about by numbers; now, numbers of men cannot be kept
together without money." Before Malthus, Steuart worried about
the relationship between the volume of agricultural production and
the numbers of the population. He is very much aware of local
agricultural surpluses, and he explains the growth of towns and
cities as necessary to form consumption markets and labor markets.
The growth of cities and the desertion of land, he remarks, give an
"additional occupation to statesmen," and thereby political economy
has become more complex.

A French economic historian, Pierre Dockès, has carefully traced
in the writings of eighteenth-century economists, especially the English and the French, the concern with the internal organization of
the national territory (which he calls "the spatial factor in economic
thought"). Such organization must always be coordinated, of course,
with the system of monetary circuits and with foreign trade. From
the works of Cantillon, Quesnay, Condillac, and Turgot, and those
of James Steuart and Adam Smith, Dockès draws an interesting
picture of the debates about urbanization and decentralization,
about the relationships between the capital city and the country at
large, and between city and rural countryside.[41] He shows how much
attention most of these economists paid to the influences of the
city and of the means of transport to the market upon agricultural
production and prices, and hence upon land use. These ideas were
carefully revived and organized into a theoretical system by the
German economist von Thünen, whose belated influence on German and American geographers has been considerable after 1930.[42]

[40] *An Inquiry into the Principles of Political Œconomy, Being an Essay on
the Science of Domestic Policy in Free Nations*, 2 vols. (London, 1767).
[41] Pierre Dockès, *L'espace dans la pensée économique du XVIe au XVIIIe
siècle*, Paris, see especially part 2.
[42] J. H. von Thünen, *Der Isoliert Stadt*, I (1826). The works of Professor
W. Braeuer, of the University of Marburg, in the 1950s, have shown how much

Von Thünen worked in the early part of the nineteenth century in a Germany still divided into many states, partitioned in terms of its economic space by numerous and involved webs of customs and tolls. A customs union was, however, being prepared, and the *Zollverein,* unifying Germany as a small "common market," was established in 1833. Such policies had been discussed since Adam Smith advocated the advantages of a liberalization of the movement of goods, and even more since the American and French revolutions had swept away the ancient obstacles to free trade within the territories of their respective countries. Fichte's book in 1800, written with a strongly political and nationalistic flavor, may well have inspired the more scholarly work by Von Thünen. Lacking large-scale overseas expansion, Germany was thinking in terms of organizing for self-sufficiency in a closed state. After some time, the late nineteenth century provided a rapid broadening of the horizons of German opportunity, and the preoccupation with isolation was postponed, to be revived after the defeat of 1918.

Perhaps Dr. Dockès would have given us an even better picture of the centuries he studied and of their economic ideas if he had not limited his analysis, especially for the seventeenth century, to authors officially recognized as economists by modern, orthodox cataloguing. Had he included, for instance, the works of such writers as Montesquieu and Jefferson, he would have obtained a fuller and more significant picture. For Montesquieu did not neglect the role of commerce, of money, and of a certain division of labor in *The Spirit of Laws,* nor did he avoid consideration of the spatial factor, even though it may not have been under the guise, so important to modern thought, of the costs of transport.

Jefferson wrote his *Notes on Virginia* first to answer a questionnaire submitted in 1781 by François de Barbé-Marbois, of the French legation in Philadelphia, who was gathering statistical accounts of the different states; then he revised and published it in response to the very great interest in this kind of description that had arisen among his friends. It is well known that the *Notes* are an excellent collection of factual information, but they are much more. The organization of the territory, the distribution of population, and constitutional representation are discussed. It is worth noticing how contemporary some of Jefferson's sentences sound when he refers to the need for reapportionment, how timely also are his remarks on education, including the need for more education in general

---

von Thünen's models were inspired by much older ones; he may have underestimated, however, the influence on Thünen of Fichte's work on the "isolated commercial state."

and the usefulness of teaching more geography to the better students. The retort to the pessimistic assessment of North American natural resources by Buffon and Peter Kalm is interesting and amusing, but still more important is Jefferson's demonstration that the decisive factors for the country's future are the quality of the people and of the system of laws, for these will determine the use of the territory by the people. That the territory remains an essential though passive element in the future destiny of the state is emphasized by the interest and care with which survey data has been gathered and presented.

Indeed, the period from the beginning of eighteenth century through the 1820s may be considered the time when our modern ideas on national territory and the tasks of government within it were formed. An incubatory period started in the sixteenth century, and the process took about three hundred years. Most historians who have written about the ideas of eighteenth-century liberals or physiocrats stress that the concepts of liberty and equality were constantly discussed and favored.

Liberty for nations as sovereign states and liberty for individual citizens of these states seemed to be the right policy, and though it might need some governmental planning, it seemed bound to produce equality also among states and peoples. Very soon, however, and especially in the debates concerning the workers of England and the common people of France, it appeared that liberty applied to economic growth was prone to produce more differentiation and less equality. The next century will raise the issue of "socialism," and liberty and equality will begin to appear locked into a dire conflict one against the other. The competition for progress did not seem to favor equality either among individuals or among regions. The issue of territory will seem to recede into the background of the theoretical debate, although it will remain subjacent to much of it. In practical politics the period from 1820 to 1950 will demonstrate on the other hand a growing and bitter concern with control of territory.

IV

Density, Sovereignty, and Happiness:
The Organization of Spatial Partitioning

THE modern way of partitioning accessible space into well-separated compartments endowed with self-government and sovereignty spread rapidly around the world after 1815. This movement progressed notably in the nineteenth century, particularly in Europe and the Americas; it gained even faster, in all parts of the world, in the twentieth century. The emergence of new independent national states is still proceeding: at least one such state, Bahrein, came into existence while the final version of this book was being written; another one, Bangladesh, emerged while the book was at the press.

In 1971 there were more than 150 independent states in the world. Most of them acquired their independence after 1918, by the division of much larger political structures called "empires": the Austro-Hungarian and Ottoman empires were divided up after World War I; the gradual dismantling of the colonial empires of Great Britain, France, the Netherlands, Italy, Belgium, Japan, and the United States produced after World War II the greater number of the new states scattered around the globe. If one considers, however, that the Peace of Westphalia of 1648 granted the status of sovereign state to some three hundred political units previously contained within the framework of the Holy Roman Empire, the total number of independent states in the world in 1970 is smaller than the number in the Europe of 1650 alone. In this interval of three hundred years a profound political evolution occurred in Europe, modifying not only the number, but also the very concept of independent statehood and of sovereignty.

In 1650 the political structure was still partly determined by the feudal and dynastic systems inherited from medieval laws and customs. In most European countries the state's body politic was not yet clearly differentiated from the person of the monarch. In 1970, the political unit is assumed to be a nation, and sovereignty is exercised in the name of the national community. This momentous change developed gradually, and most of the evolution, constitutional, social, and political, took place in western Europe and North America. It was this national state born in the North Atlantic realm and quite clearly shaped at the end of the eighteenth century, that was adopted as the model by the era of nationalism that ensued, and by the multiplying national states of the second half of the twentieth century. This national state is based on the firm, material foundation of territorial sovereignty; the dominant role of the nation is written into its laws. The emergence of this form of political organization was, however, due to definite cultural and economic circumstances, and when carefully examined, territorial sovereignty appears to have been used by the North Atlantic peoples as an instrument to achieve economic and cultural aims.

From Security to Happiness

Before economic aims could be emphasized in constitutional laws, the states of western Europe needed to achieve a fair degree of internal security: security in the physical sense both for individual inhabitants and for the political structure of the country. This required enough protection in the daily routine of life and work to assure survival and the reaping of the produce of the land; it meant, therefore, some order and policing. Imperfect as it was, the feudal order brought to people, even to those it reduced to serfdom, more security than they had been able to enjoy amid the chaos and constant migrations of the earlier Middle Ages.

As the central power of the kingdoms and of a few republics extended its authority and military control over their respective territories, the safety of the inhabitants and of their homes, movements, and stores increased. The progress of safety helped economic stability and growth; larger revenues from the territory in turn helped government to promote greater security for the people and the economy. Despite frequent wars, rebellions, and heavy taxation, physical security and economic opportunity combined, one advancing the other, to reinforce the controlling structure of the state and its territorial sovereignty. It is noteworthy that such great and rich cities as London, Paris, and Amsterdam—communities that could have afforded walls—were open cities in the seventeenth century. They were capitals of strongly constituted states whose governments were capable of providing the fundamentals of secure living in their respective territories.

Once security was assured and economic opportunity expanded, more people asked for more participation in the common wealth. They would not have dreamt of it, had their daily routine been merely one of struggling for physical safety. Having provided protection, governments had to start providing participation, more sharing out by an elite, more sharing in for the mass. Obviously, the inhabitants of the American colonies would not have been asking for "representation" and for "happiness" in the 1770s if they had not felt fairly secure in their country, among themselves and against the Indians, the French, and the Spanish. Opportunity for happiness became the overriding concern once independence and self-rule had been secured. Charles A. Beard was certainly right in emphasizing that the American Constitution was largely aimed at providing a system of economic regulation.[1]

The Americans could soon look toward the "unlimited resources" of expanding opportunity, on their continent, in overseas trade, and in a consumers market fed by large-scale immigration. The situation in Europe was different, however; even in Great Britain, the industrial revolution was not necessarily improving the lot of the mass of the people.

Writing about the enclosures of the eighteenth century, Sir Llewellyn Woodward remarked:

The procedure at every stage was weighted in favour of the large landowner. Compensation paid to the cottiers was of little use to them, since it could not buy the advantages which they had lost. The enclosure of common land deprived many thousands of small grazing rights which had kept their families just above subsistence level.[2]

Agricultural improvements forced country laborers to drift to the towns. Parliament, then dominated by landed gentry, adopted Poor Laws intended to help the proletariat thus developing in the country; but as the eminent historian of the Industrial Revolution, Paul Mantoux, put it: "the industrial revolution created a problem which even the most ingenious devices of charity could never solve. How was it possible to improve the condition of the working multitude, who had so small a share in the wealth created by their labours?"[3] This problem spread from country to country along with technological and industrial progress. It remained the essential dilemma of European politics through the nineteenth century, leading to the formulation of socialist doctrines by economists and causing civil strife and revolution. In the 1840s trouble spread repeatedly and increasingly on the continent. There were riots in various manufacturing districts of England; the brief civil war of the Sonderbund

[1] Charles A. Beard, *An Economic Interpretation of the Constitution* (New York, 1913).

[2] E. L. Woodward, *History of England* (London, 1965), p. 132.

[3] Paul Mantoux, *The Industrial Revolution in the Eighteenth Century* (first published in French in 1906; rev. ed., London, 1961), p. 440.

shook Switzerland in 1847; revolutions ripped through Italy, Germany, Austria, and France in 1848. In that year monarchy was again overthrown in Paris, Karl Marx and Friedrich Engels published *The Communist Manifesto,* John Stuart Mill published his *Principles of Political Economy,* and serfdom was abolished in Austria.

The focus was definitely on the condition of man; the doctrinal debates through the nineteenth century seemed to turn away from territorial questions: the principle of the national state with territorial sovereignty had been well established at the very beginning of that period. Now, more general problems of universal and moral portent seemed to be taking over, and the Romantic movement in literature pointed in the same direction. People believed in progress and in man's capacity to improve his condition, to "pursue happiness." For this purpose a redistribution of the products of the people's labor seemed to be the first target for policy. Could it best be reached by more freedom of economic and political activity or by more equality in rights and revenue, which would have to be controlled from above? The debate stressed intervention versus *laissez faire,* the power of labor versus the power of capital, harmonious evolution versus violent revolution, positivism versus romanticism.

The eighteenth century may claim to have established the rightfulness of the emancipation of nations; the nineteenth century strove in many ways to establish the emancipation of the individual. While the aims were economic as much as moral, the means had to be legal and political. The century began with the abolition of the slave trade on the high seas and in the British Empire and continued with the abolition of serfdom in the Austrian and Russian empires and of slavery in the United States. It opened with legislation aimed at protecting the poor, the unemployed, and the industrial worker in Great Britain; it ended with the recognition of trade union, with antitrust legislation and the first dawnings of the welfare state. Economists, political scientists, and sociologists paid little attention to geographical space in that century. It was, nonetheless, in that same time that the modern scientific discipline of geography was born, that the question of resources came to the forefront of politics (often under the name of "natural resources" or "national resources") and that a serious concern arose about boundaries and frontiers, and how to draw them.

In fact, no other century as yet drew and demarcated as many new boundaries between compartments of geographical space as did the nineteenth,[4] for while the doctrine was concerning itself with Man,

[4] Most of the lines partitioning Latin America and Africa politically, as well as a good deal of those on the map of Southeast Asia, were drawn between

the practice felt no pursuit of happiness could be effectively organized without a proper delimitation of sovereign jurisdiction on accessible territory. The territorial principle was to play an essential part in the background of two dramatic debates of that era: the debate between nationalism and internationalism on the one hand, and the debate between density and dispersal on the other. The former involved the pros and cons of sovereignty, the latter concerned environmental organization for happiness.

Spatial Organization and Nationalism

Nationalism, in its modern expression, has been built on territorial foundations, and it required a territorial base upon which the sovereignty of the nation could apply its jurisdiction. A nation may perhaps exist without being able to exercise any sovereignty, but nationalism implies firstly a claim to promote the existence of the nation as a distinct group, with a distinct system of laws, which means independence; and, secondly, it implies a promise to promote the welfare of the people, which means a set of material resources at their disposal and, if they so decide, at their exclusive disposal. It is this *right to exclude others* that could not be implemented without territorial sovereignty.

The nineteenth-century trend toward a greater number of stronger national states worked in two different ways insofar as territorial partitioning was concerned. Firstly, new states were formed by the subdivision of larger political systems. Thus Greece in 1830, Rumania in 1859, and Bulgaria in 1878 won their independence from the Turkish Empire; Belgium separated from the Netherlands in 1830; and Cuba gained independence from Spain in 1898. This process of *separation* from larger empires has continued at an accelerated rate in the twentieth century. Secondly, new states were formed by the union of several existing political units, usually national states themselves until the moment of merger. This process of *coalescence* has been less common but has led to the emergence of important powers: thus Germany proclaimed a new German Reich at Versailles after the Prussian victory over France in 1871; thus Italy unified in 1860 under French auspices.

The formation of a national state by separation is more typical of the "era of nationalities." It usually occurs when a group that

1810 and 1900. In Africa most of the states that acquired independence in the twentieth century adopted as their national boundaries lines of demarcation drawn in the nineteenth century by the European powers to delimit their various colonies.

constitutes a minority in the nation but a majority in its own region (in terms of race, culture, or religion) rises up to claim independence. The most obvious solution lies in separating from the larger system the portion of territory within which the minority group is concentrated; such was in very typical fashion the case of Greece (1830). Further difficulties have developed and Irredentist claims have been advanced when, as was the case of the Greeks, more communities of the same people, culturally and religiously, lived in adjoining or not too distant territory remaining outside the new state's jurisdiction. The resulting tensions have led in some cases to reshuffling of boundaries, in others to migration or "exchange" of population.

The expression "not too distant," in our quantitative age, may seem vague. The concept of *distance* became extremely important in politics and economics after the sixteenth century, as so much more space became accessible to human activities. However, sheer physical distance, as measured in units of a single and stable standard, soon proved to be inadequate to measure accessibility. The length of time that a voyage lasted was as important as the distance in terms of mileage, if not more. In the time of the sailing ships— that is, until the late nineteenth century—the duration of a sea voyage depended more on the winds than on any other physical consideration. The cost of overcoming the distance varied with the size of the vessels and the freedom and safety of the route. It came also to vary with the frequency of the relations between the points at the two ends of that "distance" and therefore with the degree of transactional interdependence between the places linked; cultural, technological, economic, and political considerations thus combined to determine and modify the notion of "distance."

Sheer mileage remained very important, everything else being equal, but such equality existed in practice only for a very small number of cases. With the progress of the technology of transport in speed, reliability, capability to handle larger volumes, and diversity of competing means, distance was bound to become less weighty a factor in politics. The means of transport and communication evolved very quickly after 1820: it was often remarked that to cover the distance between Rome and Paris Napoleon was still using means of transport very similar to those used by Julius Caesar, even though there had been improvements during the intervening eighteen hundred years in the design of carriages and the breeding of horses. But since the 1820s every generation of Europeans has faced new means of traffic and a new situation with respect to transportation.

Nevertheless, it was in the 1820s that the Monroe Doctrine set up a great divide in the mid-Atlantic, which proved for a century and a half more significant for the partitioning of the world than the division drawn by the Papal decrees of 1494–1506. The doctrine that two "separate systems" with distinct sets of interests existed on the two sides of the Atlantic rested to a large extent on the width of the ocean and the relative difficulty of communication between two distant parts of the world. It was partly the distance that had forced the settlers in the New World to feel somewhat autonomous. In the eighteenth century, instructions from the central government of the empire were often disregarded in the overseas possessions not only of England but also of other European powers. The "newness" of the system resulted largely from the sort of society that evolved, liberated from the shackles of inherited rights that committed, long in advance, the use, ownership, and disposal of available resources. An entirely new social structure had to arise, in each of the colonies separately, incorporating whatever native elements it needed to absorb or preserve. Different climatic conditions also affected social and cultural behavior in some details. But the appropriation *anew* by the government or by some group of large amounts of land and other resources was fundamental to the emergence of "sets of interests" that were quite distinct from one another and even more so from that of the colonizing country.

Nationalism needs some time to arise: it must have leadership and a doctrine. The colonies overseas took a while to raise their own, locally bred elites and to formulate the doctrinal tenets conveying the specific interests of the local economy and culture. Religious differences, which were fundamental from the start in many of the English colonies in America, were instrumental in bringing about the separatist tendencies. No such differences really existed in the Spanish colonies, with perhaps the exception of the Jesuit experiment in Paraguay, but local Indian cultures were more diversified and advanced than in the northern parts of the New World, and the Spanish colonies, having started earlier, formed with time influential local Creole leadership that provided the direction of their struggle for independence.

The variety of geographical situations, distance, and relative isolation concurred to cause more political partitioning of the world map. National claims were put forward not only by "oppressed" nations seeking independence and more sovereignty but also by well-established, powerful states desiring more territory, usually overseas. While in places colonial empires gave way, in other places they expanded. Some additional partitioning developed whenever any

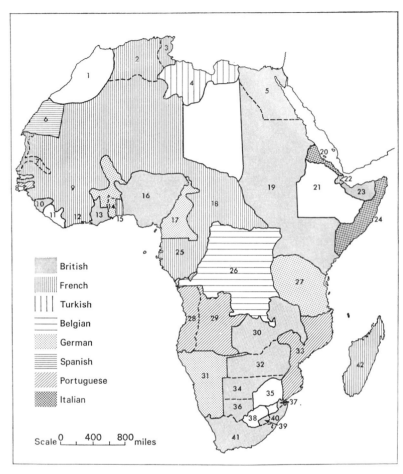

9   The Scramble for Africa: 1885–1898. *1*, Morocco; *2*, Algeria; *3*, Tunis;
4, Tripoli; *5*, Egypt; *6*, Río de Oro; *7*, Senegal; *8*, Port Guinea; *9*, Sudan;
10, Sierra Leone; *11*, Republic of Liberia; *12*, Ivory Coast; *13*, Gold Coast;
14, Togo; *15*, Dahomey; *16*, Niger; *17*, Kamerun; *18*, Ubangi-Shari; *19*,
Anglo-Egyptian Sudan; *20*, Eritrea; *21*, Abyssinia; *22*, French Somaliland;
23, British Somaliland; *24*, Italian Somaliland; *25*, Congo; *26*, Congo Free
State; *27*, German East Africa; *28*, Angola; *29*, Portuguese West Africa;
30, Central Africa Protectorate; *31*, German Southwest Africa; *32*, South
Africa Company; *33*, Portuguese East Africa; *34*, Bechuanaland Protectorate; *35*, South African Republic (Transvaal) ; *36*, Bechuanaland; *37*, Swaziland; *38*, Orange Free State; *39*, Basutoland; *40*, Colony of Natal; *41*, Cape
Colony; *42*, Madagascar. Compare with the map of present-day Africa,
p. 109.

European nation's claims of sovereign jurisdiction over territories overseas were recognized by the consensus of European powers. The most remarkable case of such distribution of "sovereignty" was the redrawing of the political map of Africa at the Berlin Congress in 1885. Most of the interior of that vast continent was unexplored and barely known to the European governments at the time, but a lively scramble for titles to the possession of African territories was developing, and was sharpening tensions between several of the contending powers. The "General Agreement" signed at Berlin in 1885 attempted a codification of the African territorial situation, with complete disregard for the existing native kingdoms and tribal organizations. The territories staked out by the European powers were recognized and approximately mapped. The tricky juridical situation of the Congo was solved by recognizing it as a "free state" with King Leopold of Belgium as its sovereign, which allowed Leopold to administer that country almost as a privately held plantation until he transferred his sovereign rights to the Belgian nation. The Berlin agreement also outlined rules for further acquisition of African territory. These rules were not always applied; boundary conflicts were frequent in Africa, as well as in the more peaceful areas whose nondemarcated boundaries were merely just sketched on maps.

European nationalisms continued with this expansion of colonial empires in the nineteenth century to affect the partitioning of the world outside Europe. Although the Monroe Doctrine had restricted to some extent the scramble for territories in the Americas, Africa and Asia offered an open field for colonization.

The triumph of the principle of independence for every nation that requested it was to come in the twentieth century. The rapid proliferation of independent states then caused the practical significance of sovereignty to evolve. The general circumstances of political organization were modified in the meanwhile, partly as a result of technological change, partly as a consequence of the emergence of "superpowers," and partly with a gradual tendency in economic thought to accept governmental intervention as a necessary policy of nationalism. The latter trend began early in the nineteenth century.

The National State and the Welfare State

Nationalism has been basically concerned with the people belonging to the national community: it wants to give these people as good a life as possible. The "quality" of life requiring security and self-government by the standards of recent centuries required a territorial compartment within which the national community assumed responsibility for her own destiny and lived according to her own system of laws. Once such a base was secured, the quality of life had to be promoted by all the means available within the territory and from outside it. The most common way of measuring quality of life was always by comparing it with the past of the community and with the way of life of other nations, especially the wealthiest and strongest of the day.

The nineteenth century introduced and made general the idea of providing *economic security* for the individual citizen, whatever his standing in the nation. This concern for the welfare of the mass was taken from the domain of charity, which had been largely in the care of churchmen in the past, to become part of the domain of economic theory and of government action. Two main streams of economic thought vied for government attention and for inspiring policy. On one hand the "liberal" school held out for free trade and the operation of supply and demand mechanisms to provide for the individual's subsistence; it offered also the opportunity of freedom and, in case of failure in such competitive circumstances, the safety device of the laws helping the poor. The other trend of thought was that of the socialists and required organized and planned intervention of the community to foster the interests of the individual. The debate over Karl Marx's *Das Kapital* spread the ideas that the individual is unable to stand up against the power of capital if he is not a "capitalist" himself and government intervention is necessary to control and regulate the money markets and the manipulation of credit.

In the early nineteenth century the liberal doctrines dominated the policies of most of those European governments that worked to improve the condition of their people. In the more advanced countries laws regulated the exploitation of workers in manufactures. England started with the Factory Act of 1802, which limited the working hours of pauper apprentices, and continued with a long series of labor legislation. The repeal of the Corn Laws in 1846, besides encouraging free trade, was aimed at preventing a shortage of food and a rise in the price of bread after the English harvest and the Irish potato crop failed in 1845. Such measures proved insufficient by the end of the century, and despite constant opposition to the principle of government interference, legislation was brought in to foster the welfare of the people.

The first domains in which governments found it necessary to bring their authority to bear on a national scale were elementary education and public health. This really started in France during the Revolution, when the government took over even the higher education system in the 1790s, and Napoleon reinforced this trend. In England the Public Health Act of 1848 forced all cities and towns to improve their water supply and sewerage; after the great cholera epidemic of 1855, when Dr. John Snow demonstrated in London that the disease spread through contaminated water, more legislation ensued on a national scale.[5]

Little by little central governments took responsibilty for services to the mass of the people of a kind that prefigured in a modest but significant way the coming of the "welfare state" in the twentieth century. These measures were not adopted in most cases to honor any socialist doctrine but rather to lessen tensions from which manufacturers and the economy suffered, to remove threats to survival, to increase the labor force and improve the performance (with the health) of the average worker. While working toward more economic security for the multitude, these laws also favored the efficiency of industry as desired by the employers. In the countries of western Europe, by the end of the nineteenth century, a certain emulation existed between governments to improve the standards of living of their people, largely through administrative interference. The liberalism of Adam Smith was left far behind by the actual evolution, and John Ruskin could, somewhat radically, castigate the author of *The Wealth of Nations* as "the half-bred and half-witted Scotchman who taught the deliberate blasphemy: 'Thou shalt hate the Lord, thy God, damn his laws and covet thy neighbour's goods.' "[6]

For practical purposes the policies advocated by nationalistic politicians, seeking to make their nation better and stronger, and those advocated by socialistic doctrinaires, seeking to improve the condition of the poor, were concurring in some domains of the domestic economy by 1900 and thereafter, while still widely differing in other areas of politics. By 1900 the French Radical-Socialist party, while still rather conservative in some respects, was favoring some mild form of "state socialism." In the 1920s and 1930s in Germany the National Socialist party of Adolph Hitler offered a

---

[5] It may be noteworthy that the Board of Health of New York, with jurisdiction over the five boroughs, was created in 1866 largely in recognition of the need for large-scale controls, thus anticipating the later consolidation of Greater New York.

[6] As quoted by Edwin A. Seligman in his Introduction to *The Wealth of Nations*, Everyman's Library (London and New York, 1964) , p. v.

synthesis of extreme nationalistic imperialism with a broad socialistic program, in some respects borrowed from Soviet policy. Italian fascism also adopted some state socialism in its policies.

The growing together of the purposes of nationalism and socialism in domestic policy[7] had the effect of considerably reinforcing the territorial concerns of politics. As they evolved toward the "welfare state," each nation felt a strong urge to take stock of the needs and resources of the people within the national borders. The authority of the government had to coincide in strict fashion with the land area that was to benefit from the welfare measures. At the same time the question arose of the capacity of a dense population, crowded on a limited territory, to achieve some sort of self-sufficiency that could compare with the "quality of life" and the average personal affluence in countries less squeezed in terms of space.

Density and the Need for Resources

The prosperity of the nineteenth century and the progress of welfare in public health and in economic aid brought about a considerable increase in the numbers of the population in Europe, despite large-scale emigration to other continents, especially to America. This increase was unequally distributed among countries. In the nineteenth century it was quite steep in England and Wales (where the population rose from 9 million in 1801 to 32 million by 1901) or in Belgium (3 to 6.7 million) but rather slow in France (28 to 40 million). This caused a substantial thickening in the density of population of most European countries. As demographic statistics improved, the crowding in some regions became better known, and its consequences began to be assessed and often bemoaned.

The nineteenth century was, on the whole, a period of industrial and economic expansion within Europe. The labor force was growing, and the growth was needed to man the proliferating industries. Moreover, overseas settlement, proceeding apace in various parts of the world, attracted some of the population surplus. However, grave concern with the threat of overpopulation had been voiced at the very beginning of the period, when Malthus published his famous *Essay on the Principle of Population* (1798), in which he demonstrated that population increase could in the long run easily outgrow the expansion of resources, particularly of agricultural production. There was in his view a direct relationship between the number of

[7] This was well brought out by David Thomson in *World History: 1914–1961* (Oxford, 1963).

people and the total volume of the harvests reaped from a limited land area, and as the former rose faster than the latter the threat of famine appeared at the end of the projection. Population increase was in theory unlimited while land area and its produce were finite. The answer offered to the problem was control of population in the world as a whole and in its different parts to establish some degree of self-sufficiency.

But the time was one of expanding space, of improving agricultural yields, of rather general optimism, and of strong belief in the lasting supremacy of the white European stock. Though Malthusian ideas were repeatedly discussed, particularly in Protestant countries, no serious concern about a general scarcity of resources arose in political circles until the twentieth century. Some of the more forward-looking Europeans then realized that a feeling of anxiety about resources and about their political destiny was coming to European nations.

Alexis de Tocqueville forecast the rise of the Russian and American nations in the famous Conclusion to the first volume of his *Democracy in America:*

> All other nations seem to have nearly reached their natural limits, and they have only to maintain; but these are still in the act of growth. All the others have been stopped or continue to advance with extreme difficulty; these alone are proceeding with ease and celerity along a path to which no limit can be perceived. The American struggles against the obstacles that nature opposed to him; the adversaries of the Russian are men. . . . The conquests of the American are therefore gained by the plowshare; those of the Russian by the sword. . . . The principal instrument of the former is freedom; of the latter, servitude. Their starting point is different and their ways are not the same; yet each of them seems nominated by a secret design of Providence to hold some day in their hands the destinies of half the globe.[8]

Tocqueville insists in all his works that social and political organization is the fundamental cause of differences in strength and happiness among nations. His forecast about the Russians and Americans, so much quoted after 1945, appears however to have something to do with territorial status: the other nations, he says, "have nearly reached their natural limits." Tocqueville was well aware of the geographical lore of his time; the first chapter of *Democracy in America* is a geographical description of the United States with references to the writings of Jefferson, Alexander von Humboldt, Con-

---

[8] *La démocratie en Amérique,* I (Paris, 1835) This and subsequent quotations from the Conclusion are in my own translation from the recent very good edition of 1948.

rad Malte-Brun, and William Darby. In his Conclusion he saw the United States and Russia as having at the disposal of their rapidly increasing populations the resources of an already acquired but yet largely empty expanse of territory. Tocqueville compares the area and the density of population of Europe and the United States: on the basis of the work of the geographer Malte-Brun, Tocqueville estimates the average density of Europe in the 1830s at 410 inhabitants per square league; postulating a land area for the United States equal to three fourths of that of Europe, he foresees that, reaching a similar density, the American nation will number about 150 million people, who will all be "equals, belonging to the same family, having the same starting point, the same civilization, the same language . . . and among whom thought will circulate in the same form, displaying the same colours." Such a massive and homogenized nation would be in Tocqueville's opinion an entirely new phenomenon, the consequences of which were hard to grasp.

The quality of Tocqueville's forecasting appears indeed amazing. The population of the United States reached 150 million by 1950, when the power of the united American nation was at its zenith. It is interesting that through the medium of the size and density of population Tocqueville brings out the role of territory. His reasoning assumed that the American nation has at her disposal a vast territory to expand upon, practically empty or barely settled by any other population. This is almost spelled out in the last paragraphs of his first chapter, where he concludes the geographical description of the continent by writing off the role of the Indians for all practical purposes. Tocqueville does not develop his view of the population and territorial characteristics of Russia; only a footnote hints at the rapid growth of the Russian population. He apparently expects his French readers to be better aware of Russian than American geography. However it is striking that in the cases of the two nations that he saw so clearly advancing toward what our epoch has called "superpower" status, Tocqueville gave so decisive a part to the availability of vast territorial expanses to settle and develop.

The unity of government and the "common starting point" were of course essential in his mind to insure the cultural and political unity indispensable for the massive structure and weight of these nations. He does not expect China or the Latin American republics, already independent in his time, to measure up. He detects an element of equality and homogeneity in Anglo-America that is decisive to his thinking. It is surprising that in 1835 he may have expected the Russian nation also to acquire such characteristics, but Russia was of course the new and dominating power on the continent of

Europe after 1815, and the forecast of a great destiny for her was then less surprising than for America. In both cases Tocqueville seems to have appreciated the continuity in one piece of these two nations' territories. The colonial empires scattered in different parts of the world appeared less likely (as the American example had demonstrated) to produce a real unity of national culture and way of life. Also, the availability of more space for development next to the already settled areas is a factor in his reasoning. The advancing "frontier" of settlement, as described by Frederick Jackson Turner in the 1890s, would be an element first in the feeling of expansion and greater future for the whole nation, and second in the process of unifying the various immigrant components and insuring the abundance of land and resources to be shared, all of which Tocqueville considered necessary to obtain equality among the citizens.

Both America and Russia were certainly remarkable in the nineteenth century for the vast spaces within their national boundaries open to a frontier settlement and contiguous to the older territorial base of the nation. In his *Politische Geographie* (1896), the German geographer Friedrich Ratzel stressed three main characteristics of states from a geographical point of view: the space or territory (*Raum*), the location (*Lage*), and a curious, psychological feature he termed the "sense of space" (*Raumsinn*); the best-developed example of this "spatial sense" was the American nation, and one may well think of Ratzel's *Raumsinn* as related to F. J. Turner's frontier.

The territorial scramble among the world powers reached its greatest intensity at the turn of the century; to the scramble for Africa, which was about completed when the French Protectorate was established over Morocco (1912), should be added the redistribution of territories in the Far East, where the United States took over the Philippines, France Indochina, and Japan Formosa and Korea. World War I again put into question the balance of power in the world and led to another redistribution of territories at the expense of the former German, Austro-Hungarian, and Turkish empires, mainly affecting Central Europe and the Middle East. At the Paris Peace Conference of 1919, President Wilson had asserted the principle of self-determination for national communities in a way that greatly helped new independent states to emerge through the ensuing half century.

It was in the period between the two world wars that international politics became especially concerned with the problem of population density, that is, of the quantitative relationship between the number of people and the area of territory under their jurisdiction. Several powers complained of being *overpopulated,* and the debate grew bitter in the 1930s. They meant that their national territories were crowded to the point of lowering, in their opinion, the standard of living and the national per capita income. This overpopulation was the basis of claims that more territory should be made available to these nations, then called the "have-nots" by contrast to the richer nations, possessing more territory per capita, and then called the "haves."

The differentiation between the two categories was politically clear: the "have-nots," Germany, Italy and Japan, had strongly nationalistic governments and were asking for *more,* more territory (including of course the population therein) and more resources. Population density figures and trends were much bandied about at the time of the debate. Taken by themselves these figures were inconclusive: the "have-nots" had relatively high average densities, but not as high as those of Belgium, the Netherlands, and Great Britain, classified among the "have" nations. A refinement in the notion of population density consisted in calculating it not as inhabitants per square kilometer of territory but as inhabitants per square kilometer of arable land; such calculations for the early 1930s produced the following figures: Japan, 993 inhabitants per sq. km. of arable land, the Netherlands 802, Great Britain 800, Switzerland 772, Belgium 640, Brazil 639, Norway 412, Austria 349, Italy, 307, Germany 305, and so forth.[9] The definition of "arable land" is also highly debatable: it changes with the techniques applied and the investment put into the soil; what a backward economy may consider nonarable soils could well become arable in more expert hands.

Density could not be clearly related to standard of living or to level of income. High densities in rural districts, often encountered in the Far East or in Egypt, usually spell misery, while similar densities in more urbanized districts, especially in Western countries, corresponded even in the 1930s, a period of worldwide economic depression, to rather high incomes per capita. A rather clear relationship has been established between miserable living conditions and high population density in a closed, localized economy, although a population of similar density may live in relative affluence in a wide-open economy. These rules were well demonstrated by geographers such as Albert Demangeon and Pierre Gourou in the 1930s, and the experience of the post-World War II period confirmed them. Demangeon concluded his study of overpopulation by pointing out that the question was largely psychological and subjective: besides the cases of certain crowded regions of Asia, where dire poverty

[9] According to Albert Demangeon "La question du surpeuplement," *Annales de Géographie,* no. 266 (March 1938), 113–27.

proved "overpopulation" in their kind of economic organization, it was almost impossible to determine scientifically the condition of overpopulation. It could be ignored by people satisfied with a low standard of living, and become the subject of political tension among people asking for a higher standard.[10]

The "have-not" powers accused the "haves" of keeping for their own benefit the markets and produce of their vast territories, including their colonial empires. To compensate for their own lack of resources at home, the "have-nots" were requesting more and better colonial possessions (for instance, the vast expanse of desert then controlled by Italy in Libya and Somalia would not satisfy the Italians, who embarked on the conquest of Ethiopia and the annexation of Albania). They also wanted more access to sources of raw materials in areas outside their jurisdiction. Japan invaded China and announced the scheme of forming under her control a "Greater East Asia Co-Prosperity Sphere." When in 1939 Germany attacked Poland, World War II broke out in Europe.[11]

After World War II the dispute between "haves" and "have-nots" was soon forgotten. The "have-nots" lost the war and had little to claim. The new economic doctrine, which prevailed under American leadership, emphasized the differences in the levels of economic development among countries around the world. The countries of rather backward economy were called first "underdeveloped" and later, more optimistically, "developing countries." Policy and planning adopted on an international level aimed at getting the better developed countries to help the "developing" ones to catch up in terms of their agricultural and industrial resources.

In the debate about density and resources the concept of territory showed once more that it is the *organization of a territory by its population* that counts more than any other feature of it. The territory must be the physical base and support of the organization, and the latter should be adapted to territorial circumstances. These circumstances include the general economic policies that make the inhabitants more ambitious for progress or more satisfied with the *status quo*. One is thus reminded of Plato's statement that "the territory should be large enough for the subsistence of a certain number of men of modest ambition and no larger" (see above, p. 17).

Territorial circumstances also include the policies isolating a

---

[10] *Ibid.*, pp. 125–27.

[11] The dispute about population density, territories, colonies and raw materials was carefully studied in the various reports prepared for the conference on "Peaceful Change," the Tenth International Studies Conference, held in Paris in 1937.

country in terms of trade or providing for it the role of central hub in a large-scale trading network. Plato of course advised isolation (on an island, away from the sea) to avoid political involvement with the outside. The twentieth-century "have-nots" attempted officially some isolation and autarky in order to prepare themselves better to strike out for conquest and expansion. The post-World War II experience of broadly expanded, freer international trade and economic development in a world increasingly subdivided into a greater number of independent national states has been more rewarding. In this new framework even Germany, Italy, and Japan have been able, with more numerous populations than in the 1930s and much higher densities, to develop new resources in strictly limited territory, thus giving higher living standards and more happiness to their peoples. It now appears necessary to turn to the contemporary situation in terms of political partitioning and to assess the relationship that may exist between size, density, and the happiness of the people.

Size and Density among Nations

The dismantling of the large colonial empire caused a proliferation of new national states. By 1970 there were in the world 140 self-governing sovereign units, according to the United Nations register. The shape and extent of their territories appear to have often been determined for former colonies by the boundaries drawn in the past by the colonial powers, either in agreements between themselves to delimit their respective possessions or as a result of internal decisions to delimit territorial subdivisions within those possessions that were held in large chunks of territory.

It is remarkable that so many administrative lines, drawn some time ago, and in some cases a long time ago, for purposes of purely administrative jurisdiction, have been accepted on the whole by dozens of various new national states as their international boundaries. This phenomenon will have to be examined later, when we come to discuss the internal structure of modern states. As the present political map stands, a great variety of sizes (in terms of land area or population) can be found among recognized states.

Considering the land area of independent countries, we may say that today large states are those covering more than one million square kilometers (i.e., about four hundred thousand square miles). There are twenty-seven such states today. It is interesting to rank them by size of land area, with their figures of population and density, to appreciate the diversity, quantitatively measured, of modern states (see table 1). The ranking by area does not corre-

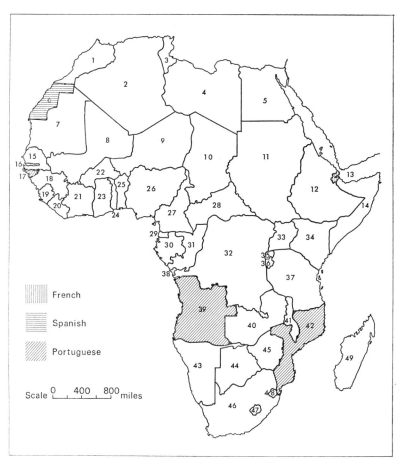

10 Present-Day Africa: the Proliferation of National States, *1*, Morocco; *2*, Algeria; *3*, Tunisia; *4*, Libya; *5*, United Arab Republic; *6*, Spanish Sahara; *7*, Mauritania; *8*, Mali; *9*, Niger; *10*, Chad; *11*, Sudan; *12*, Ethiopia; *13*, French Territory of the Afars and the Issas; *14*, Somali Republic; *15*, Senegal; *16*, Gambia; *17*, Portuguese Guinea; *18*, Guinea; *19*, Sierra Leone; *20*, Liberia; *21*, Ivory Coast; *22*, Upper Volta; *23*, Ghana; *24*, Togo; *25*, Dahomey; *26*, Nigeria; *27*, Cameroon; *28*, Central African Republic; *29*, Río Muni; *30*, Gabon; *31*, Congo Republic (Brazzaville); *32*, Zaïre (or Congo–Kinshasa); *33*, Uganda; *34*, Kenya; *35*, Rwanda; *36*, Burundi; *37*, Tanzania; *38*, Angola; *39*, Angola (Portuguese); *40*, Zambia; *41*, Malawi; *42*, Mozambique; *43*, South-West Africa; *44*, Botswana; *45*, Rhodesia; *46*, South Africa; *47*, Lesotho; *48*, Swaziland; *49*, Malagasy Republic.

Table 1. Size of contemporary states (1968)

Rank by size	Name	Land area (1000's of sq. miles)	Population (in millions, 1968 estimate)	Density (inhabitants per sq. mile)
1.	U.S.S.R.	8,649	237.0	29
2.	Canada	3,851	20.0	5
3.	China	3,691	730.0	198
4.	United States	3,615	201.0	55
5.	Brazil	3,286	88.0	26
6.	Australia	2,967	12.0	5
7.	India	1,261	523.0	416
8.	Argentina	1,072	23.0	23
9.	Sudan	967	14.0	16
10.	Algeria	919	13.0	13
11.	Zaïre	905	16.0	18
12.	Saudi Arabia	830	7.0	8
13.	Mexico	761	47.0	62
14.	Libya	679	2.0	3
15.	Iran	636	27.0	42
16.	Mongolia	604	1.2	2
17.	Indonesia	575	113.0	197
18.	Peru	496	12.0	26
19.	Chad	495	3.5	8
20.	Niger	489	4.0	8
21.	Mali Drvenik	478	4.0	10
22.	Ethiopia	471	24.0	52
23.	South Africa	471	19.0	42
24.	Colombia	439	20.0	44
25.	Bolivia	424	4.0	10
26.	Mauritania	398	1.1	3
27.	United Arab Republic	386	31.0	83

SOURCE. United Nations statistics or estimates and United States *Statistical Abstract 1970* (for square miles measures). Colonial dependencies are not accounted for.

spond at all either to the ranking by population or to the ranking by thickness of population density.

Six sovereign states appear much larger than all the others: the Soviet Union with over eight million square miles is in a category by itself, and five other countries extend over areas of three to four million square miles each. Among these, four have been formed in recent centuries by a process of colonization directed from Europe, and the majority of their inhabitants are of European stock: they are Canada, the United States, Brazil, and Australia. Only one of the six very large states, China, is the result of very old settlement and political organization developed in that same territory for several thousand years, though the general contours of the boundaries have been shifting substantially during that long span of time. Although third in area, China is undoubtedly the most populous state on earth,[12] and her average density, though not among the higher, was in 1968 triple the world average (which stood at sixty-eight people per square mile). As a mass of population having characteristics of unity, culturally and politically, China is the largest and most ancient nation. Among the smaller states large enough to be included in table 1, Iran and Egypt (now called the United Arab Republic) are two other cases of very ancient and rather unified states, regional poles of political organization. India, while a culturally distinct area, has known a much more shifting and less unified political past. The Soviet Union can claim to have held for several centuries, in full independence, the main bulk of her present territory, since the Russians claimed and colonized Siberia; the Russian settlement, however, spread out from the central "rivers and forests" state in eastern Europe toward the Black Sea and the Pacific, by systematic colonization, only in the sixteenth century.

In the second category of area sizes on table 1, among the states now covering between 750,000 and 1,300,000 square miles, only India, the largest, may claim a long political past in her subcontinent and an ancient local cultural tradition. The other six states in that category, from Argentina to Mexico, are recent creations, having broken away from European colonial empires in five cases and from the Turkish empire in the case of Saudi Arabia. One could also argue that Saudian boundaries, and therefore the extent of a territory largely made of empty desert, have been determined since 1927 by agreement with Great Britain whose possessions or protected lands then surrounded most of Saudian territory. Sudan, Algeria, and Zaïre are three recent states, each of them enclosing vast areas almost devoid of population, and all three resulting in their outlines from the scramble for African possessions in the nineteenth century.

The last category of table 1, the states ranking fourteenth to twenty-seventh in size, remains within the dimensions of 380,000 to 680,000 square miles. With the exception of Iran, Mongolia and Ethiopia, and perhaps that of the U.A.R., because of the ancient antecedents of Egypt, they are all products of the subdivision of colonial empires.

There are some 112 other, smaller sovereign states. The majority

[12] This is the United Nations estimate; even with a plus or minus variation of 100 million people, China would still be far ahead of India.

are less than 130,000 square miles in extent (that figure approximating the area of Finland or Italy). The European powers that played such a leading part in history for at least one thousand years are rather small in area: France, the largest of them, covers 211,000 square miles; Great Britain, 94,000; Spain, 195,000; Portugal, 35,500; Sweden, 173,000; the Netherlands, 13,000. Twenty states cover less than 10,000 square miles each, and some of them play a substantial role in their respective regions of the world: thus Israel, El Salvador, Luxembourg and Singapore (which covers only 224 square miles). Obviously the extent of the territory tells little about the actual strength and role of the country in the international arena. Many of the recently created independent states are very small (Bahrein, Kuwait, Mauritius, Malta, Trinidad, Jamaica, again Singapore, and others), but some are very large, although they may have been cut out of desert areas. Such is the case of a good many of the African and some of the Asian states listed in table 1: Libya, Mongolia, Chad, Niger, Mali Drvenik, and Mauritania have less than five million people each in spite of the huge areas of land each covers, and their population density hovers between two and ten per square mile.

In some cases, where the population figures look more impressive, the country still encompasses a few rather small but thickly populated districts, and much more empty space; such are the cases of Algeria, the Sudan, Zaïre, and even Australia, Canada, Peru, and Brazil.

In fact every one of the twenty-seven larger states on table 1 holds within its territory some desert regions due to aridity, cold, or tropical rain forest. The United States is no exception, and neither is India despite her very high average density of 416 per square mile. In a large territory the distribution of population is *always* very unequal. With the growth of large cities and metropolitan regions, the concentration of a large proportion of the population on small fractions of territory has increased.

The size of a nation may be better measured by the number of people than by the land area. If the round figure of 100 million may be adopted as the minimum standard for the large nations of today, we counted seven of them in 1968: China (730 million) and India (524) were far ahead of all others; the U.S.S.R. (237), the United States (201) form another group; and three other Asiatic countries form a third group neighboring on 100 million: Indonesia (113), Pakistan (109), and Japan (101). The last two do not appear among the larger countries in table 1. Another category, between 50 and 90 million people, would include six or perhaps seven nations:

11 Present-Day Europe. The national states of Europe in 1970. *N*, Netherlands; *B*, Belgium; *A*, Albania; *C.H.*, Switzerland. Compare with maps on pp. 42 and 85.

Brazil (88), Nigeria (62), the Federal Republic of Germany (60),[13] the United Kingdom (55), Italy (52), France (50); perhaps Mexico (47 and a high rate of natural increase) ought to be added to this category, after which the population size of nations drops below 35 million. There is a large category of old and new nations (19 of them) in a medium size, between 15 and 35 million, and then a majority of states below the 10 million mark. It is noteworthy that among the present 140 sovereign states only fourteen, one tenth of their total number, have about 50 million people each or more. The total population of the world was estimated in 1968 to be about 3,500 million, so that an average for 140 states would have stood at 25 million, half of the minimum size used above and one fourth of our standard for the larger nations. The fourteen larger nations together accounted for 70 percent of mankind. Only thirty-three nations had 15 million or more people, and about one hundred comprised less than 10 million. In fact thirty-three states had less

---

[13] If counted together as one nation, East and West Germany would total 77 million.

than 2 million people each, and some of these smaller nations were listed among the larger in area on table 1.

The recent proliferation of statehood caused in the patterns of partitioning of space and of people a puzzle and a fragmentation that may have been desired in a time when self-determination was widely applied, but it certainly also encouraged the frittering away of sovereignty. How could a nation of a few million people or even less exercise effectively the jurisdiction of sovereignty over a vast territory of hundreds of thousands of square miles? Perhaps a few people could police vast spaces with the help of abundant and highly automated modern equipment, but this required the support of a large economic machinery supplying the financial means, a rather unlikely prospect for a small number of isolated people. Policing is, moreover, only one of the attributes of sovereignty but hardly its major purpose. We are thus brought to consider the matter of the density of population.

As could be expected from the preceding comparison between the rank-size order in terms of area and in terms of population, a great diversity is to be observed among the states in the variation of density: the lowest densities are close to 2 per square mile as in Mongolia; the highest figure among independent states is that of Singapore, which reached 8,900 per square mile in 1968 and must be close to 9,000 in 1971. This is however the average for a total population of only 2 million occupying 224 square miles. If we considered only more substantial nations, of the 10 million size or more, the record of population density would appear to be disputed between the Netherlands (985 per square mile in 1968) and Taiwan or the National Republic of China (972 in 1968). The Netherlands has long held one of the higher densities among recognized nations; the crowding of their territory was already described by seventeenth-century writers. Conversely, Taiwan (or Formosa) had in the past the reputation of a rather thinly populated island; massive Chinese immigration during the recent half century has increased the density rapidly.

If we look at the list of very densely settled countries around the world, we find on it mainly territories small in area and always in *maritime* locations, often insular. The following countries belong in the very dense category: Singapore, Malta, Mauritius, the Netherlands, Taiwan, the Maldive Islands, Bahrein Islands, Belgium (819), South Korea (803), Japan (710), West Germany (627), the United Kingdom (590), Trinidad and Tobago (517), Ceylon (473), Italy (455), Jamaica (455), Haiti (437), India (416), East Germany (409). Stopping at the 400-per-square-mile mark in 1968, this list

testifies to the predominance of maritime locations. The Netherlands and Belgium were so deeply penetrated by maritime trade
early in the Middle Ages that they may in many respects be likened
to a delta, almost an artificial assemblage of isles and peninsulas.
The highest density for a multimillion population, though not on
self-governing territory, is now Hong Kong (an island plus a scal-
loped peninsula), the population of which (4 million people) aver-
ages 10,000 per square mile in the present limits of the Crown Colony. The only truly continental exceptions in the list are the two
Germanies and the enormous mass of India. Among the seven larger
nations in terms of their total population the record density is that
of Japan (an archipelago) followed, though at a considerable interval, by India.

Japan is considered today one of the richer nations on earth. In
1968 her gross national product per capita reached $1,404 (against
$350 in 1958). It was the highest of any sizable nation outside Eu-
rope, North America, and Australia. In 1968 the GNP per capita
stood at $4,379 in the United States, $3,000 in Canada, $2,154 in
Belgium, $1,980 in the Netherlands, but $312 in Taiwan and only
$80 in India. High or low density may correspond to any level in
availability of resources. It is the social and economic structure of
the nation and the equipment of the territory, not the extent of the
land, the size of the population, or its density that determine the
comfort and happiness of the people.

The statistical and historical data on the preceding pages may,
however, bring out one important relationship between density and
territory: the frequency with which maritime location is associated
with thick density. The fact is quite well known and has been often
pointed out; on a world map of population density almost all areas
of higher density are found along the periphery of continents, the
interior of which appear, as a general rule, less densely populated,
although exceptionally, there are small inland patches of quite dense
settlement. The insularity of most very thickly settled states under-
scores these observations.

To explain this pattern one must acknowledge the difficulty for a
very dense population to subsist and to thrive in a self-sufficient
economy, within a small territory. A relative lack of local sources of
supply (especially in terms of food and raw materials) can be compensated by foreign trade. Transport and trade have in the past
been easier by sea when large volumes of goods were to be handled:
bulky cargoes are more easily and cheaply carried in ships by sea;
the "ocean stream" is a great highway leading to a variety of markets either for buying or selling; and finally, the "ocean stream" has

always been freer for trade and transport than was any itinerary over land. Even before the freedom of the high seas was proclaimed and generally accepted, it was more difficult to police maritime spaces than land or river transport networks strewn with tollhouses and other controls.

Population density is therefore related to large-scale trade networks. It has always been so. Plato knew it when he advised in his *Laws* that the number and the ambition of the people be kept down in order to avoid the evil forces of traders, merchants, and seamen that could interfere with the political life of the community. He also wanted the population settled inland, away from the shore and from maritime influences. This matter of the population density has never been separable from the matters of location and of foreign trade.[14]

The open and the closed societies constantly interplay with the open and closed maritime horizons. These horizons were restricted for early medieval Europe, where life and economics were quite localized, while the energy of people was spent in local wars, in the struggle to survive, and on the universal matters of faith. The Crusades, the Mediterranean expansion, and then the great maritime discoveries opened up a new era, in which territories had to be partitioned, density rose, sovereignty strengthened, overseas trade expanded, and materialism grew. The national state was organized as a springboard for and a defense against the territorial scramble.

The formation of density, however, has reached in the twentieth century a mass and an acceleration that could hardly have been visualized in the past: the total population of the globe was estimated in 1650 at 545 million, in 1800 at 900 million, in 1900 at 1600 million, in 1968 at 3,500 million. It had more than doubled in these two thirds of the twentieth century. Projecting this accelerated rise, statisticians could foresee a population of 7000 million by the year 2000.[15] Density had to increase with the total number in a limited land area. It had to increase faster in some districts than others un-

[14] It is curious that studies aiming at determining an "optimum" level of density have mainly blossomed in periods of slackening international trade, and in nations looking for an economy of self-sufficiency. This was the case among statisticians of central European countries in the 1930s. See the bibliography in Demangeon, "La question du surpeuplement."

[15] Recent changes in the birth rates in several Western countries, especially the United States and France, have led to some questioning of the accuracy of such forecasts. It is interesting to remember Demangeon's listing of the variety of opinions among experts in 1937: Carr-Saunders predicted doubling of world population in 60 years, Knibbs in 70, Kuczynski in 110.

less a generalized dispersal accompanied the evolution. With urbanization, it was in fact the concentration of people in small selected districts that occurred. Much higher and increasing densities have become the rule in this century, and these trends are considerably influencing the organization and the significance of territory.

Urbanization and the Use of Space

Most states large in area have empty regions. All states, small or large, have an unequal distribution of population. New technology and automation have considerably reduced the personnel who must be employed on the spot for agricultural, mining, and even manufacturing production. Population from the rural countryside and small scattered towns moved to larger cities. Urbanization proceeded apace and is still going on. By 1800 there were four cities in Europe and four or five in Asia reaching the half-million size or more: London, Paris, Constantinople, and Naples in Europe, Peking, Canton, Bombay, Edo (Tokyo), and possibly Shanghai in Asia. By 1900 there were forty-two cities of about that size or larger, and today there are more than two hundred. A United Nations report estimated the total population of cities of more than 500,000 was 106 million in 1920, 350 million in 1960 and will reach 730 million by 1980. The great Japanese architect Kenzo Tange has suggested that as 1900 was the age of the metropolis of one million inhabitants, 1960 was the age of cities of 10 million, and the year 2000 will be the age of "cities" of 100 million people! Cities are overflowing their municipal limits, growing toward one another, coalescing into conurbations or huge urbanized regions such as the "Megalopolis" along the northeastern seaboard of the United States that I described in 1961.[16]

By 1970 conurbations of the 10-million size numbered about five: New York, London, Tokyo, Shanghai, and Paris; perhaps the urban region around Los Angeles could be added as a sixth case. Other such widespread agglomerations were forming around Chicago, São Paulo, Peking, the Ruhr, and Moscow. Still much larger but quite dense urbanized regions, of a looser and more irregular weave, were forming on the megalopolitan scale, that is, encompassing about 40 million people at average densities above 750 per square mile. Such a density is today often observed in towns or small cities of North America. It is also found to be the average density for entire nations: in fact we saw the Netherlands, Belgium, Taiwan, not to

[16] Jean Gottmann, *Megalopolis* (New York, 1961).

mention smaller states like Singapore and Malta, already populated at higher *average* densities. The coming of Megalopolitan regions, agglomerating on rather continuous territory such high densities for masses of more than 40 million people in each case, could be observed in the 1960s in several places on the globe: in the Megalopolis of the northeastern United States from Boston to Washington, in the Tokaido region of Japan between Tokyo and Kobe, in the northwestern lowlands of Europe, outlining a triangle from Calais to Amsterdam to the Ruhr; and even in England between the southeast coast and Merseyside.

It was in the context of the formation of huge urbanized systems that Kenzo Tange, projecting to the year 2000, may have envisaged "great cities" of 100 million people. One may dispute whether the concept of "city" would still apply to such huge agglomerations, despite their continuity in urbanization. But the fact of living and working at such high density for very large numbers of people is new and pregnant with organizational consequences. Immense human agglomerations at high density have also achieved, especially in Europe and North America, a rather high average level of economic affluence. The consumption of goods and services of the urban populations rose to very substantial quantities per capita. The large city of today, even a conurbation of one million or less, requires enormous volumes of goods to be moved in and out, an intense traffic of people, and a great variety of diverse services. To keep such a large, affluent city functioning the local environment must be equipped, organized, and maintained in an extremely involved and efficient way.

It is not our purpose here to describe or analyze the organization of the urban environment, but it is essential to realize that such large cities cannot function simply by "good neighborliness" and by small private enterprise. Public health and sanitation must be organized and controlled by large-scale authority. Means of transport, communications, water and power supply, and many other fundamental needs of the large urban community must be planned and provided for by large organizations, strictly controlled. A city could not survive the prolonged breakdown of these services. The American way of life has succeeded in maintaining a very important component of these organizations in the domain of private enterprise. Many such enterprises have grown to be giant corporations, and their size, comparable to that of a whole national economy in some cases, owes much to the size and complexity of the market they serve, or, to use a term which has become current in the American business jargon, it owes much to the character of "their territory." Territory thus acquires the meaning of area to be serviced and from which benefits are derived, even though it is not under the exclusive jurisdiction of the business organization, and may well be a field open to competitors.

The formation of high density has brought about large-scale organization. Even in the domains left to private enterprise in North America, public authority has established some controls and claimed regulatory jurisdiction. The more urbanization, industrialization, and affluence increase, the more regulation is needed for the environment and for the organization of society. In the United States these controls and regulatory powers have been established and exercised by a great variety of agencies belonging to three tiers of governmental organization, local, state, and federal. In European countries there has usually been more centralization of authority and more interference by public agencies in the control and servicing of the economy.

The progress of urbanization does not affect only the territory properly urbanized and its regional environment. Obviously these large agglomerations can exist and function only in close symbiosis with various outside areas. They receive supplies from some regions and send their products to others, and they get especially involved with the activities of other large urban regions, partly because they exchange goods and services between such agglomerations, and partly because the necessity to compete in many fields and to coordinate their activities in many others leads to more contacts and exchanges of people, ideas, and information.

Thus emerges a general picture of increasing complementarity and interdependence, as well as rivalry between different regions within a country and between cities or related regions located in different countries. The use of space grows more specialized. A division of labor works itself out between regions and countries to a certain extent, but it must be regulated. The concentration of employment and population is resented in the areas consequently thinned out, though these less densely occupied regions may remain or become essential components of a more diversified, mechanized, and automated economy. To maintain a nation as a going concern while accepting the process of fluidity, subdivision, specialization, and inequality among its various parts, political authority must concern itself with economic problems on the national as well as the regional scale. It must interfere through planning and regulation at least; and in some countries, depending on their political philosophies, the central government will assume all the functions of economic management. The latter solution, mainly applied in the communist countries, leads to dire authoritarianism, as all the tools of political and economic power are gathered in the same hands.

In the middle of the nineteenth century Karl Marx, Friedrich Engels, and most of the socialist theoreticians expected the capitalist society to crumble away because of the evils and inequities they saw developing in the cities and in urban slums, and because of the concentration of wealth and power already apparent in the major financial centers. Successful communist revolutions occurred in fact in the twentieth century in countries of rather backward economy, little urbanized, industrialized, or capitalized. Lasting communist regimes, built upon socialist doctrines, were established and ruled in Russia after 1917, in China after 1949, and in other countries of underdeveloped status at the time of such takeover. The aim of authoritarian planning in those countries was to catch up with the more advanced Western capitalist nations, first in terms of industrialization and technology and then in terms of standard of living and popular opulence. No such equalization has yet been reached between, say, the United States and the Soviet Union, but both have shown considerable concern with the diverse evolution of the various regions of their respective territories. Both have endeavored to make the various regions specialized, complementary, and well coordinated, both among themselves and with respect to the other competing or related regions of the world outside their borders.

Territorial organization has been complicated and diversified by the advances of urbanization. Governments have had to concern themselves even with the distribution of population density inside their borders. In authoritarian regimes all migratory movements are supposed to be officially controlled, though some trends seem to have developed beyond the plan, such as the growth of Moscow and its suburbs since 1945. In the more liberal countries the governments have assumed less strict regulatory powers. The freedom of movement about the national territory is one of the basic constitutional rights of the citizen in most of the countries of the West, especially in the United States, the United Kingdom, and France. But incentives may be offered to orient geographically the trend in one direction while discouraging similar trends in other directions. More stringent planning authority has been granted to special public agencies in terms of land use. One could debate the degree of efficiency in the enforcement of land-use planning policies in the various countries. Higher density and the fear of "running short of land" or of agglomerating too many people in a few conurbations has led such "crowded" countries as the Netherlands and the United Kingdom to apply strong controls in matters of land use and industrial location. However, some of the neighboring nations with quite comparable densities, such as Belgium and West Germany, have not applied controls so severe.

The same technological evolution that determined the concentration of population into urban agglomerations also considerably improved the productivity of agricultural land. In western Europe during the last fifty years, urbanization proceeded parallel with the growth of agricultural production and with the shrinking of the total area of actually tilled land. Locally some regions may have experienced an expansion of urban land uses (including land uses for the needs of transport) which threatens them with running short of space. This is the result, on the local scale, of a dilution of the density of land utilization either for industrial or for residential purposes; but on the national level, with very few exceptions, urbanization has devoured less space than has been thinned out by the shrinking of the spatial needs of agriculture. Most west European countries have been able to *increase* their lands under forest while urbanization proceeded. This trend has been clearly noticed on the margins of the large metropolitan regions: around the megalopolis in the northeastern United States, around Paris, around Munich, and even in some parts of England and of Japan.[17]

The rapid changes in the geographic and economic structure of so many national territories, in consequence of the progress of urbanization, have been one of the major forces driving modern politics into concerns of a territorial and a geographical nature. Moreover, the higher densities of urban living have caused other modifications in the demand for space. Firstly, urban residential densities were very thick at the end of the nineteenth century, even in the most prosperous countries; some lowering of these densities by deconcentration of habitat and urban sprawl has been necessary. In the older cities of Europe, residential densities within city limits of fifty to eighty thousand per square mile are still common. A century ago, in the larger cities, such densities commonly ranged from one to two hundred thousand. Today such figures may be found in the crowded and spreading cities, bursting with slums, of the less well developed countries, especially in Asia and South America.

The usual American metropolis (New York excluded) holds residential densities between ten thousand and thirty thousand per square mile. In Southern California this figure falls to five thousand and less. The dilution of density consumes much space. As a large city sprawls out, distances lengthen between places of residence and

[17] See my remarks in *Megalopolis*, chapters 5 and 7, and in Jean Gottmann *A Geography of Europe*, 4th ed. (New York, 1969).

places of work, shopping and recreation. To join all these specialized parts of the same metropolitan body together more time and space must be taken up by the traffic between them; and the planning of the physical and financial networks involves more space and more governmental participation, on both the local and national levels.

The greater affluence of society causes constant increases in the per capita consumption of space for residence, for work, for transport, for recreation. When this rising consumption of space develops in conditions of low density and therefore of abundance of land, the major governmental concern will be to supervise the financial operations involved. When on the contrary such needs develop in conditions of high density, scarcity of land, and general multifaceted crowding, governmental regulation and interference becomes necessary with every aspect of land use and community organization. The happiness of the people today rests on all these aspects of territorial and environmental control. Sovereignty must thus manifest itself in jurisdictional fields from which it seemed to have withdrawn during the period of liberal economic thinking in the eighteenth and nineteenth centuries. The happiness of a *denser* community would appear to require a greater and more constant exercise of sovereignty over the territory that must be serviced for the community's needs.

The realities of the time point to some extent in that direction, and the political process therefore pays increased attention to territorial organization. At the same time, however, other consequences of the same technological progress and of the same social and urban trends have unleashed very different forces working toward a dilution of sovereignty as defined by territorial bounds. The significance of territory, once again, is rapidly evolving in the second half of the twentieth century, in search of a new order.

V

Crossroads and Frontiers amid Modern Fluidity:
The Shifting Demands on Territory

THE concept of territory has steadily evolved through the centuries. Organized society partitioned the space it used into political units, each with its "territory." That word was too often interpreted to mean a certain extent of land and water delimited by lines agreed upon between neighboring political authorities. Examined more closely, the concept appears to designate rather a relationship established between a community of politically organized people and their space. Juridically it was jurisdiction that defined the territory; politically it was the area within recognized boundaries (although frontiers and boundaries have been frequently questioned, challenged and redrawn) ; in political geography it was a base of operation and as such a shelter. To take on a valid general significance, a definition of territory must be "relational."

The Stages of the Territorial Concept

The very nature of this relationship between the people and their space, and its significance to the practice and the doctrines of politics, have varied through recorded history as we have sketched it in the preceding pages, at least for the Western world; they varied slowly, gradually adapting to the changing demands made on accessible space. The people occupying a piece of land constantly strived to establish a system of relations with that area that would make it a homeland providing protection and the means of survival. This being achieved, the territory had to be at least the base for the "good life," whatever the definition of the term, which certainly evolved and we assume progressed in the last seven thousand years. Several essential turning points must be recognized in the slow and difficult path of history.

First *the formation of density,* which Gordon Childe called the urban neolithic revolution, and which was probably the great change reported by Homer and Aristotle when people gathered into groupings of "several villages united in a single complete community."[1]

---

[1] Aristotle, *Politics,* 1. 2. 1252b; this was the great change, "for they lived dispersedly, as was the manner in ancient times" before the *polis* was constituted.

This was the origin of the city-states in Mesopotamia, Anatolia, Greece, and along the Nile and Indus rivers. The conglomeration of population had the decisive result of bringing about communal life and hence the need for law and an authority to enforce it. This was particularly imperative in dry or drying-up climates, such as those of the Middle East: people congregated around the remaining sources of fresh water, particularly in the valleys of the streams that kept flowing across the desiccated lands, the Nile, the Euphrates, the Indus. Water and irrigable land were scarce commodities, and their use had to be regulated. Interdependence developed between downstream and upstream settlements lest the latter consume all the available water, denying the former the quantities they needed. To coordinate this use, territorial planning arose, based on water resources. Larger scale political organization was thus born in desert conditions; more dispersed, smaller city-state territories could be considered satisfactory under the less barren conditions of Europe, including Greece, in the early stages of history. The unification of Egypt as one monarchy, and of the kingdoms of Mesopotamia and Iran, probably corresponded to economic needs that imposed an environmental organization on a larger territorial scale.[2]

The second turning point comes with Alexander the Great and his grand design, perhaps suggested by Aristotle, announcing the principle of *universal imperium*. Within the empire, there had to be subdivision into provinces, and it developed into political fractioning as, after Alexander's death, his Generals established dynasties in the provinces, which fought among themselves. But a general notion of the vast Hellenistic world had appeared, soon taken over by and assimilated into the Roman Empire. The fall of the imperial Rome of the Caesars did not seem to affect territorial jurisdiction: Constantinople was a second Rome, and the basileus was another Caesar; then with Charlemagne the empire was reborn in the west and under the aegis of the Pope, the pontiff in the Eternal City. In the east the caliphs claimed another sort of universality, another holy

See V. Gordon Childe, *Man Makes Himself* (New York, 1951)), especially chapter 7.

[2] This is convincingly shown by Henri Frankfurt, *The Birth of Civilization in the Near East* (Bloomington, Ind., 1951); see also V. Gordon Childe, *Man Makes Himself* and Emile-Felix Gautier, *L'Afrique blanche* (Paris, 1938). Frankfurt reminds us that "The ancient Egyptians said that Menes, who first ruled at This, brought the whole land under his control. They designated him as the first king of a first dynasty and thus unequivocally marked the unification of their land as the beginning of their history" (*op. cit.*, p. 78).

empire; and so did, in a third part of the world, the emperors of China. In Europe, however, complex processes were at work through the Middle Ages, and around 1500 A.D. another crucial stage was reached. A few strongly constituted kingdoms in the west of Europe were delineating territories, each with a national identity long fought over: France, England, and Spain. The Renaissance, the Reformation, and the great maritime discoveries combined to create a situation in which kingdoms had enough centralized authority to provide their subjects with essential protection; and they could do so because the central authority was capable of procuring the financial means, while also opening up vast opportunities in the new lands and seemingly unlimited resources overseas. Personal allegiance, the basis of medieval protection, lapsed gradually between the sixteenth and the eighteenth centuries, and the national allegiance of the people to the sovereign state prevailed. Protection and opportunity were now provided to the community behind defined boundaries under a distinct system of laws. The American and French revolutions claimed natural frontiers and independence for nations that were drafted into armies to defend their own sovereignty and in which Church and state were separated. Their distinct national personalities had legal and territorial roots. The concept of the national state's exercising territorial sovereignty was accepted and spread across the continents as the model of political organization. By 1920 one could sense the forthcoming dismantling of remaining empires and the "final" and formal division of accessible space into such national compartments.

Indeed only the high seas and the air space above them remained unappropriated sections of accessible space. The Antarctic was subdivided into areas claimed by various powers, although the United States refused to recognize such appropriation of the enormous and unoccupied icecap. The partitioning and organization of air space, which was claimed above the territory to the infinite as soon as men flew in aircraft, was consistent with the usual treatment of any newly accessible sector of space. In 1494, long before any limits had been reached, Spain and Portugal claimed sovereignty over the new lands they had just started to discover for as far as the space might extend. The Allied Powers did the same in affirming the principle of air-space sovereignty in the international conventions of 1919 and 1944.[3]

[3] On the history of airspace appropriation before 1946, see John C. Cooper, *The Right to Fly* (New York, 1946). As Cooper points out, "although the United States did not ratify the Paris Convention of 1919, it definitely asserted its sovereignty over its airspace in the Air Commerce Act of 1926, the Civil

By 1970 a motley carpet of independent sovereign states had been thrown over most of the planet. Few territories were not self-governing; these were under the sovereignty of some power of which they were dependencies. Some further subdivision remained possible in recently constituted States afflicted by inner strife or tension; some cases of unification also seemed possible between a few contiguous countries. Still, increased partitioning has been the trend of the century; despite regional groupings developing along lines that respected the sovereignty of participating countries, the separate territorial base had become the rule and the privilege of every people that could demonstrate its capacity to operate as a distinct national entity.

It was significant that the Holy See in Rome had felt it necessary to ascertain its independence from the Italian national state (into which the Papal States had been incorporated after 1870) and to exercise some token temporal power through the recognition of the Vatican City as a separate sovereign entity (since 1929). With its 109 acres the Stato della Citta del Vaticano is the smallest territory of a sovereign power. In a very different development, which had, however, also a religious background, a Jewish state was established in Palestine as the independent and sovereign state of Israel (1948). Its territory was then shaped, after bitter fighting, by armistice lines drawn under United Nations auspices with the neighboring Arab countries. It was then said that the map of Israel resembled a drawing by Picasso more than a normally constituted territory. Three hundred years after the Peace of Westphalia religious differences were still partitioning the world and claiming territorial bases.

The movement toward statehood and national sovereignty, begun in the sixteenth century, seems to have achieved its apogee. Is the twentieth century going to stabilize this long sought-after and disputed pattern of territorial appropriation and administration? It would then be necessary and certainly worthwhile to define the present status and significance of territory. The momentum of history has not yet dissipated, however, and in certain respects the twentieth century appears to be only one more stage in an evolutionary process, although perhaps an essential turning point. The sovereign state, based on exclusive territorial jurisdiction, may have been the evolution's purpose from the sixteenth to the mid-twentieth century. By 1970 sovereignty has been by-passed, and a new

---

Aeronautics Act of 1938 and the Pan American Convention signed at Havana in 1928. At the International Civil Aviation Conference in Chicago in 1944 there were notoriously many disagreements. But no-one questioned the right of each nation to control its own airspace."

fluidity has infiltrated the recently shaped map of multiple national states.

The Demise of the Shelter Function

Several fundamental functions of territorial sovereignty have recently been challenged and may hardly be held to operate any longer with the same results as in the past. First, the function of protection is now gravely questioned. With the development of aviation all the ancient value of land and sea frontiers was brought under a new light: spanning land and sea alike, moving at much higher speeds than surface vehicles, the man-controlled aircraft posed entirely novel problems to national defense. World War I was to prove the offensive capacity of aviation. World War II demonstrated it with much greater force, adding at its conclusion the new weaponry of the nuclear bomb delivered by air. Since 1945, extremely powerful nuclear weapons, capable of destroying almost all life within a radius of fifty miles or more from the point of impact, have been fitted not only to long-range planes circling around the globe but also to rockets which may fly half of the earth's circumference at speeds and altitudes making effective defense highly problematical. Insofar as rockets carrying H-bombs may be launched from pads located at the antipode of the target or from submerged nuclear-powered submarines plying the high seas and roving under the Arctic ice, any point on earth may be destroyed by weapons sent from almost any other point. In that situation little remains of the sheltering role of territory controlled by its national government within well-demarcated boundaries. A state with a smaller area becomes more vulnerable as the bombs grow bigger.

The technological developments which led to the present situation in the domain of offensive weaponry started a long time ago, perhaps even as far back as the legends of Icarus and of Prometheus. The invention of gunpowder and artillery were steps forward on this path. Then, in 1784, shortly after he had witnessed near Paris the first balloon flight of Montgolfier, Benjamin Franklin wrote to a friend:

It appears, as you observe, to be a discovery of great Importance, and what may possibly give a new turn to human Affairs. Convincing Sovereigns of the Folly of wars may perhaps be one effect of it, since it will be impracticable for the most potent of them to guard his Dominions. Five thousand Balloons, capable of raising two Men each, could not cost more than Five Ships of the Line; and where is the Prince who can afford so to cover his Country with Troops for its Defence, as that Ten Thousand Men descending from the Clouds might not in many places do an infinite deal of mischief, before a Force could be brought together to repel them.[4]

In 1909 the Frenchman Louis Blériot, took off in an airplane from the French shore of the Channel and landed in England, making the British realize that invasion of their island by air was becoming possible. The first international aviation conference met in Paris in 1910 and discussed the right of a state to deny foreign aircraft access to the airspace above its territory; a few years later all the major powers agreed upon the national sovereignty over their respective airspace. World War II started the use of long-range rocketry as Germany struck from the continent at targets in England with the unmanned V-1 and V-2 bombs; then in 1945 the U.S. Air Force dropped atomic bombs on Hiroshima and Nagasaki, bringing about the capitulation of Japan. In the twenty-five years that followed, this sort of technology made great progress: bombs grew bigger and deadlier; rockets improved in range, speed, and precision. Physicists have been discussing for almost thirty years now the possibility of firing defensive rockets that could meet the offensive rockets of an enemy and explode them in space. As early as 1942 scientists wondered about the possibility of accelerating offensive rockets faster than the decision to parry could be accelerated.

This new arsenal of weapons, undreamt of even by military experts fifty years ago, requires an enormous industrial machinery and a large and highly-qualified personnel. Nevertheless the United States and the Soviet Union have both developed it on a scale sufficient to destroy one another thoroughly and therefore to deter aggression by either of them or by any other power that may acquire the capability to launch such an offensive. Three other powers, the United Kingdom, France, and China, have nuclear armaments and some means of delivery. None can compare theirs, however, to the "firing power" of the two superpowers; and the partitioned world lives under the umbrella of the mutually deterrent capacity of only two nations. The situation of mutual deterrence, and the probability of annihilation of human activity and possibly all life over most of the continents if nuclear war were fully unleashed, obviously call into question the usefulness of territorial sovereignty in terms of the protection of the inhabitants.

The bigger and the more numerous the bombs, the wider the area they will irradiate lethally. The smaller the territory, the less hope it has to avoid full annihilation if encompassed in an attack. The

---

[4] As quoted by Cooper, *The Right to Fly*.

greater the concentration of population on small fractions of the territory, the easier it will be for a nuclear attack to destroy these essential components of a country, even of a large one. The present trends of proliferation of national states (creating a large number of states small in area or population) and of urbanization, which concentrates population, both concur to increase the effectiveness of nuclear war. The smaller size of states and therefore of their relative economic means is bound to restrict the possibility of creating and maintaining an adequate nuclear arsenal for their own use.

One comes to understand why shortly after the first A-bombs were exploded in 1945, the U.S. secretary of war, Henry Stimson, wrote: "Mankind will not be able to live with the riven atom, without some government of the whole." The great physicists of that time spoke eloquently: Albert Einstein of world government, Niels Bohr of a "completely open" world, and J. Robert Oppenheimer of "a world which is varied and cherishes variety, which is free and cherishes freedom . . . but a world which, with all its variety, freedom and change, is without nation states armed for war."[5]

In fact, the abundance of missiles with nuclear warheads around our planet is only one of the ominous changes that threaten to melt the sheltering capacity of territorial sovereignty like a cake of ice in the sunshine. Other technological advances applicable to warfare looked extremely promising: the chemistry of lethal gases, the cultivation of lethal bacteria and viruses. The major powers admit having stored quantities of biochemical and bacteriological weapons adequate to wipe out a large proportion of mankind. The recurrent need to do away with some of the surplus stocks occasionally causes problems that arouse the attention of the press. While in the last quarter of a century most of the world has lived in conditions of relative peace among nations, despite the persistence of a few theaters of localized warfare, mankind lived, for the first time, amidst an environment powerfully loaded by men with the means of quick and rather complete annihilation.

Perhaps it is the knowledge of the power and closeness of the ghost of death hovering above us that has kept more conflicts from erupting. But all the major nations have worked steadily toward achieving at least the basic tools of advanced modern technology, most of which could be applied to civilian as well as warlike uses. The progress of rocketry and of astrophysics has led the two superpowers on the path of one of the oldest dreams of men: reaching for access to the moon and the planets of our solar system. American

---

[5] Both quotations in this paragraph are from Oppenheimer, *The Flying Trapeze: Three Crises for Physicists* (Oxford, 1964), pp. 60–65.

astronauts have made several trips to the moon, bringing back rock samples and other observations. The Soviet Union has sent unmanned instruments to the moon. Both superpowers put many artificial satellites in orbit around the earth, some of them forerunners of manned stations or platforms that may turn around our globe for prolonged periods, during which crews may shuttle between them and the earth.

Most of the satellites are small and unmanned but equipped with instruments that make observations and send records back to earth. Some of these observations are concerned with meteorology and geophysical phenomena. Others survey portions of the earth's surface. The technology of photography from satellites and the transmission and interpretation of the images have been perfected to such a degree that detailed maps can be drawn from the data procured by satellite observations. These maps can show the lay of the land, land use, and even the quality of the crops and the traffic on highways; they can record minute changes in the landscape. Satellites can supply information comparable to that gathered through "intelligence" networks. It becomes increasingly difficult to prevent countries capable of orbiting adequately equipped satellites from "spying" on other countries over which the orbiting trajectory passes.

The sort of security and privacy that territorial sovereignty used to assure, behind the protection of solidly organized boundaries, is now waning. Several countries besides the two superpowers acquired in the 1960s the capacity to orbit satellites for various kinds of observations and for communications. Still the total sum of these remains small in comparison to the squadrons of instruments sent into space by either the United States or the Soviet Union.

When the Soviet Union placed her first *Sputnik* in orbit in October 1957, a new sector of space became accessible to man-made instruments: the interplanetary space beyond the airspace. A new chapter opened in politics, international law, and political geography. One of its first consequences was a direct challenge to the principle of the sovereignty extending in the column of space above a territory to the infinite. The Soviet Union protested vehemently when they brought down an American U-2 plane that had been making photographs of their territory while flying over it at great height without their permission. This, they felt, was violation of their territorial sovereignty; they felt free, however, to orbit first unmanned and then manned satellites over the territory of various powers that had not given permission for such overflight.

The matter could well have been raised earlier. Since the German rockets began to fly over substantial distances, carrying powerful weapons, the prospect had loomed of long-range missiles crossing the airspace or, higher up where there is no atmosphere, the sector of space above the territory of sovereign states. Would such passage violate territorial rights? One could imagine a conflict erupting between two widely separated powers, and fought with long-range missiles, which normally follow a great circle route between two points on the earth's surface. Various territories located between the belligerents would be flown over; besides the violation of space sovereignty, there is the danger of the unexpected fall of a missile. Could such passage be construed normally as "innocent passage" of the kind that custom authorizes for foreign ships in the territorial seas of a power? The risks involved in a mechanical failure resulting in a fall would disqualify such passage for the "innocent" quality, all the more so as the military objectives pursued by such passage could hardly be reconciled with the assumed neutrality of the countries lying in intermediate locations under the missile's trajectory. The recurrence and frequency of such passage would add to the view that the space so travelled was deliberately used for the political purposes of the missiles' originator.

The conclusion points rather unavoidably to the need of establishing somewhere in high altitude a "ceiling on sovereignty."[6] International law has now debated the matter rather fully: the new term *outer space* has emerged as distinct from *airspace;* at least two different storeys are thus recognized above the earth's surface: airspace, which would still be under the sovereignty of the subjacent territory, and outer space, which would not be. In fact, American policy on the matter as formulated after the adoption of a resolution on outer space cooperation by the United Nations Assembly, on December 20, 1961, rests on two principles:

1. International law, including the United Nations Charter, applies to outer space and celestial bodies.
2. Outer space and celestial bodies are free for exploration and use by all states in conformity with international law and are not subject to national appropriation.[7]

[6] I suggested that such an eventuality will be forthcoming when reviewing Cooper's *The Right to Fly;* see Jean Gottmann, *"De l'organisation de l'espace aérien"* in *Annales: economies, societés, civilisations* (1948), pp. 371–73; and idem, *La politique des états et leur géographie* (Paris, 1952), pp. 7–9.

[7] See Richard N. Gardner, "Cooperation in Outer Space," *Foreign Affairs,* XLI (January 1963), 344–59. Also, J. E. S. Fawcett, *International Law and the Uses of Outer Space* (Manchester, 1968).

The text sounded somewhat like a new edition of Grotius's *Mare Liberum,* and outer space became a sort of "high seas" free for all beyond the limits of a "territorial air space." Where would these limits be set? John C. Cooper offered at one time the rather elusive formula that sovereignty should extend in height as far as "the control" of the subjacent power.[8] Such a rule could create considerable inequality among powers, some more capable of producing tools for long-range control than others. It would also fluctuate with improvements in technology and might ultimately reach very far out, as far as the moon, and certainly into interplanetary space. More stable and objective lines of delimitation have been suggested (such as the "Von Karman line"), leaving each state a rather broad strata to exercise its sovereignty in. The matter is still far from stabilized. A new debate has arisen with the use of commercial satellites for communications purposes (of which the American-sponsored COMSAT was the first). Rockets may come into civilian use for long-range delivery of mail and cargo. All this will involve the access to outer space through a layer of airspace ruled by national sovereignty. How much the exercise of the latter will have to be regulated by common consent of all participating nations remains an open question. By 1970 only two powers have been effectively using, cooperating in and competing in outer space. The number of states or groupings of states that will achieve such capability will undoubtedly increase. Common use will require more regulation.

If the coming of a ceiling on sovereignty in altitude may remind us of the distinction, fully accepted only two hundred years ago, between the high seas and the territorial seas, the evolution of the search for resources in and under the sea has caused since 1950 a revision of the basic rules used for the public law of the sea. The boundaries of sovereignty are shifting here too, involving a reconsideration of the extent and meaning of territorial rights over maritime space. The continental shelf adjacent to a power's land territory has been placed under its sovereign jurisdiction for the purposes of economic exploitation. Conflicts about fishing zones beyond the territorial waters in adjacent seas have led to more tension and debate; and some countries now claim jurisdiction over the sea to a considerable distance (such as two hundred miles) from their shores. If such claims were to become general, and if means of access were found to mineral and other resources from the sea or the seabed and its subsoil at increasing depths, the claims

---

[8] See John C. Cooper, "The Rule of Law in Outer Space," *American Bar Association Journal* (January 1961), pp. 23–27.

recently laid to the continental shelf would extend farther out, appropriating in fact parts of what have been considered the free spaces of the high seas.[9]

Some shallow seas such as the North Sea and the Baltic Sea, the Persian Gulf and the Gulf of Mexico, have been completely cut into sections like apple pie and apportioned to the riparian powers for the discovery and use of the natural resources of the subsoil and the seabed of the contiguous continental shelf.[10] The United Nations Geneva Conference on the Law of the Sea produced in 1958 an International Convention which has been generally approved. Where the shape of the seabed caused irregularities in the continuity of the continental shelf under the sea, as along the Norwegian coasts in the North Sea, the states in the area still usually agreed to a "median line" between their shores, delimiting boundaries on the shelf and disregarding topographic features.

It would seem that, while sovereignty is being considerably diminished for certain practical purposes by some advances in technology, such as satellites, other advances have spurred the extension of sovereignty into areas, especially maritime areas, from which it has formerly been excluded. It is possible that much maritime space will soon be appropriated to various nations, though some freedom of navigation will be preserved by limiting in international law and custom the exclusive privileges of national sovereignty as previously defined.

Advancing in some ways, retreating in some others, territorial sovereignty is undergoing a significant modification. The change is even more substantial, though of a subtle nature and less measurable, in the economic relations between nations. The abandonment of most of the dreams of national or regional self-sufficiency and the expansion of large-scale and long-range international trade, regulated by international agreement, may be recognized in the future as even more potent factors of interdependence among national territories than the threatening advances in the technology of war. As

[9] For general data on recent evolution see C. John Colombos, *The International Law of the Sea*, 6th ed. (London, 1967), especially chapters 2, 3 and 4. Also Ian Brownlie, *Principles of Public International Law* (Oxford, 1966), especially part 4, and Lewis M. Alexander (ed.), *The Law of the Sea: Offshore Boundaries and Zones* (Columbus, Ohio, 1967).

[10] The United States proclaimed such a policy for the continental shelf in 1945. Pakistan annexed the continental shelf contiguous to its coast in 1950, following various proclamations of Persian Gulf states in 1949. The discovery of substantial oil and gas deposits under the North Sea in the 1950s accelerated the trend. See also Jean Gottmann, *A Geography of Europe*, 4th ed. (New York, 1969), pp. 126–33.

the extent of territorial sovereignty shifts, it may be helpful to look at it in terms of the new functions and values acquired by boundaries delimiting territory.

The Changing Nature of Boundaries and Frontiers

The English language has developed a certain distinction between the two terms that are used to describe the limits of territories: *frontier* and *boundary*. Some authors, espec ally in Britain, have used both words as interchangeable. In the American practice a distinction has been made systematically which corresponds to the meanings of both words as defined also in t ie *Oxford English Dictionary*: *boundary* is "the limiting line"; *frontier* is rather "the part of a country that borders on another," and the word is also used to denote "the borders of civilization." In French *frontière* usually means "the boundary line," though it can also be used in the sense of "a border zone,"[11] and the same would be true of *Grenzen* in German. In most languages a word exists designating the population settled along the border, which is assumed to have some specific characteristics and rights that do not apply to the people living further inland on the same territory: *frontiersmen, frontaliers, Grenzleute*. This would imply that *frontier* connotes in all these tongues a concept of zone, containing some population rather than just a concept of geometrical line.

At present an international boundary means a well-delimited line agreed upon by the countries on both sides. There is a considerable literature on the international boundaries and frontiers, largely due to geographers, lawyers, and a few statesmen.[12] It appears in reading it that the precise delimitation of territories by

[11] This was also my conclusion in the chapter "Les frontières et les marches" in *La politique des États et leur géographie*, pp. 121–45. The medieval terminology had developed the notion of "march" as a fortified (or disputed) borderland between two countries. The Germans had several countries called "Mark"; the French spoke also of "marches" in this sense.

[12] See especially Julian Minghi, "Boundary Studies in Political Geography," *Annals of the Association of American Geographers*, LIII (1963), with an excellent bibliography, and the section on "Boundaries and Frontiers" in R. E. Kasperson and J. V. Minghi, eds., *The Structure of Political Geography* (Chicago, 1969), pp. 126–60. Especially important older works are: Lord Curzon, *Frontiers*, Romanes Lecture (Oxford, 1908) ; S. Whittemore Boggs, *International Boundaries* (New York, 1940), and "National Claims in Adjacent Seas" in *Geographical Review* XLI (April 1951), pp. 185–209; Paul de Lapradelle, *La frontière* (Paris, 1927); J. R. V. Prescott, *The Geography of Frontiers and Boundaries* (Chicago, 1965).

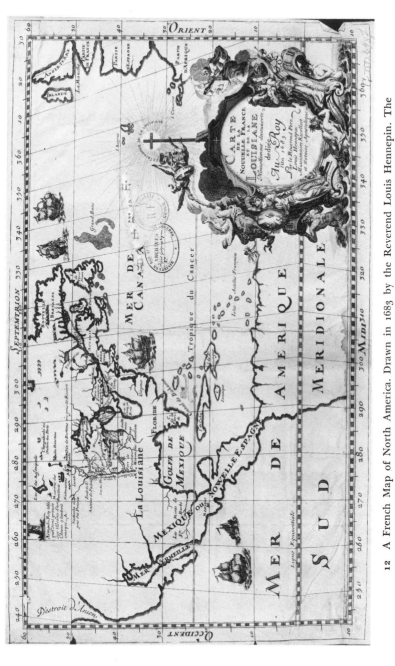

12 A French Map of North America. Drawn in 1683 by the Reverend Louis Hennepin. The continent was as yet little explored or partitioned; compare with 1750 map 13. Courtesy Bibliothèque Nationale, Paris. Photo S.P.B.N.

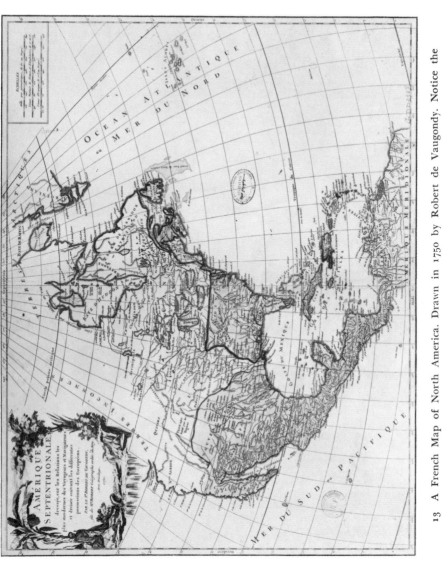

13 A French Map of North America. Drawn in 1750 by Robert de Vaugondy. Notice the progress made in the exploration and the political partitioning of North America by comparing with Hennepin's 1682 map. The boundaries have now become important and

agreement of the riparians was a rather rare occurrence until national sovereignty became important enough to make territory a precise concept, and this came about gradually in Europe in the half century after 1648. Such careful delimination as was done for the heirs of the Carolingian Empire at the Treaty of Verdun seems to have been exceptional. In the feudal system the overlapping notions of lordship, suzerainty, and sovereignty left much demarcation indefinite. The Roman Empire's famous *limes* was a front of defense of the empire against the peripheral barbarians rather than a limit line; it was organized in depth and was therefore more a zone than a line, though occasionally marked by a "wall" such as Hadrian's Wall along the northern frontier of England. As Paul de Lapradelle has pointed out,

> The problem of the modern frontier, a delimitation of equal jurisdictions, is inconceivable in the imperialistic stage of a powerful and solitary State. . . . Neither the Roman Empire nor the Frankish Empire had any conception of the modern boundary. The *Limes imperii* is not the result of an agreement, even an imposed agreement, but a mere voluntary halting place . . . a conception of the modern boundary, presupposing equal jurisdictions, could be applied only in the interior of the imperial framework, and not at its periphery.[13]

The advent of the sovereign national state gave a clearer significance to the boundaries that marked off the limits of the territory. S. Whittemore Boggs carefully surveyed the international boundaries as they partitioned the world on the eve of World War II, when the meaning of territorial sovereignty seemed clear, definite, and exclusive of any other jurisdiction.[14] Few land boundaries have lasted long. In Europe the most lasting frontier of some substantial length is probably the transisthmic boundary between France and Spain along the high range of the Pyrenees. Another, much shorter, is the strip of marshland between the Groningen province of the Netherlands and the German areas to its east. The high range of Himalayan crests marking the northern limit of India has been another rather stable boundary. The physical quality of certain areas as obstacles to movement has had something to do with the stability of these historical partitions, but there were other factors keeping some sort of balance of power on the two sides of the belt of difficult crossing, whether a lofty range, a wide marshland, or an arm of the sea.

Today the boundaries have seen their functions considerably re-

---

[13] Paul de Lapradelle, *La Frontière*, pp. 25–26 (my translation).
[14] S. Whittemore Boggs, *International Boundaries*.

duced, although all the same functions continue to operate in principle. The proliferation of independent states has considerably increased the total length of international land boundaries. Boggs calculated their total length in 1937 at 165,013 kilometers (or 102,-534 miles) .[15] It would be somewhat more difficult to give a precise figure as of 1970, but it has at least doubled. A few of the boundaries listed in 1937 have been erased; for instance, the land boundaries of the Baltic states of Estonia, Latvia, and Lithuania, absorbed after 1945 into the U.S.S.R., or the line dividing the island of Sakhalin between Japan and the Soviet Union until 1945, or the boundary separating in the past China and Tibet, or the boundary separating Canada from Newfoundland (Labrador). So much more frontier line has been recognized, however, since 1945 that we shall not try to list or measure it. It is striking that most of the new ones, especially in Africa, follow the internal subdivisions of former colonial empires, as they did to some extent in Latin America after the independence of the Spanish colonies (see above pp. 76–77). Some of this stability may be due to the care with which the former colonial administrations outlined jurisdictional provinces to keep together within one unit peoples that were relatively good neighbors and related among themselves. The drawing of some of these lines was also made easy by the vast empty spaces separating the main and not-so-numerous major nuclei or formations of density into obvious geographical and cultural units.

A large proportion of the total length of the boundaries now recognized (though not always fully agreed upon and demarcated) between distinct sovereignties in Africa, South America, and Asia extend in sparsely populated and little-surveyed regions, where the bordering states seldom have a practical reason to manifest their authority. Since Algeria, for instance, became independent in 1962 and inherited vast expanses of the Sahara Desert because these had been explored and administered by the French from headquarters in Algerian cities, Morocco has occasionally recorded some doubts as to the never fully demarcated boundary between Moroccan and Algerian territories in the southern desert parts. Many other such examples could be noted in the Amazonian basin, in the wilderness of the Congo River basin, and elsewhere.

Mapping from air photographs can lead to demarcation on paper. The actual situation in the field itself does not matter as long as population of some density of occupancy for the purpose of exploiting a valuable local resource does not arouse conflicts of interests that cannot be resolved without clearcut territorial jurisdic-

[15] *Ibid.*, Appendix A.

tional limits. Nobody was claiming the continental shelf beyond territorial waters before oil and gas deposits were shown to be accessible there and worth being tapped. Once such interests came into the arena, the continental shelf was quickly appropriated in terms of territorial sovereignty. No attempt was made to organize the use of such resources on an international basis. However, under the concessions, laws, and taxes of the state that claims the "territory," the minerals extracted are handled, processed, and distributed by various corporations of diverse nationalities through wide and multinational industrial networks. Accessibility and opportunity are great factors in the changes occurring in territorial appropriation and occasionally in the shifts of international boundaries.

Economic factors of this kind are especially important in rather empty or thinly populated territory. Where organized people maintain a presence of substantial density, the human organization (social, cultural, religious, and political) becomes the decisive factor to determine boundaries and their stability.[16] Despite an obvious divorce between religion and politics, religious diversity still plays a part in the political organization of space. Most of the prolonged conflicts involving military operations since 1945 in the various parts of the world have included a religious component, although religious differences were not the only important points of dispute. This may have been observed in Vietnam, in the Arab-Israeli conflict, in Algeria, in Nigeria during the Biafran war, and so on. Religious fanaticism has certainly been greatly moderated in recent times in most countries, but religious differences lie at the basis of cultural features which are fundamental to the behavior of people. Giving up some of these cultural traits is even more difficult for most communities than giving up territory. They prefer to migrate rather than to melt into the mold of an "alien" culture. And in the inheritance of culture the religious background still carries momentum. When a minority group seeks to affirm its cultural integrity it often takes on a territorial expression if and where the geographical distribution of the dissenting groups allows for it.

Discussing the frontier in history, Owen Lattimore brought out powerfully the role of boundaries as partitions between communities adhering to somewhat different social systems:

Frontiers are of social, not geographic origin. Only after the concept of a frontier exists can it be attached by the community that has conceived it to a geographical configuration. The consciousness of belonging to a group,

[16] This was already my conclusion in *La politique des États et leur géographie* (1952) and it was agreed to by Charles de Visscher in his *Theory and Reality in Public International Law*, trans. P. E. Corbett (Princeton, N.J., 1957).

a group that includes certain people and excludes others, must precede
the conscious claim for that group of the right to live or move about
within a particular territory.[17]

The differentiation between territories seems to become more and
more precise as society progresses and gets more "structured." This
has not been a steady evolution in history, however; territorial administration had more definite provincial jurisdictions in the Roman Empire than were left in the rather united but chaotic Christian Europe of the Middle Ages. In the second half of the twentieth
century the increasing significance of frontiers and boundaries
seems to have reached an apex in legal and geographical terms, but
a dilution of the effectiveness of sovereignty points toward a very
different evolution, seemingly in contradiction to but in practice
rather consistent with or complementary to the proliferation of national statehood. The more small or weak states there are, the more
they all need collective security of some sort.

The frontier is of less consequence to a nation where it passes
through rather empty land. This is now increasingly the case in the
interior of the massive continents. Boundary controls will thus be
concentrated at main points of entry—seaports, airports, and so
forth. The frontier is a partition, that is, *a screening instrument in
the organization of accessible space.* It screens and to some extent
controls the movement into and out of the territory. We saw that
it lost much of its military screening potential with the advent of
the modern technology of air power, rocketry, and astronautics. But
it also lost by international agreement much of its power to control
migration and the movement of goods as the liberalization of trade
and travel developed since 1950. The immense growth of international trade during the last twenty years cannot be overestimated.[18]
It has made every nation in the world more dependent on the out-

17 *Studies in Frontier History* (Oxford, 1962), p. 471. The paper "The Frontier in History" reprinted in that book was first presented to the Tenth International Congress of the Historical Sciences, Rome, 1955.

18 Figures shift fast and are not always as comparable as they may seem; however, it was significant that from 1960 to 1969 the foreign commerce (of goods
and services, imports plus exports) of the United States rose from 52 to 99
billion dollars, while the foreign trade (goods only) of the United Kingdom
rose from 2 to 3, of France from 1.1 to 2.7, of Canada from 0.9 to 2.2, of Norway
from 0.2 to 0.4. See also Saul Cohen, *Geography and Politics in a World Divided*
(New York, 1963), in which the author sketches and maps the categories of
nations more or less open on the outside through their dependence on foreign
trade. In these terms the United States appeared as an "inwardly-orientated
country" in 1960; it was less so by 1970 if foreign trade was taken as the essential
yardstick. The actual "orientation" of a country is a more complex matter.
Nevertheless, imports as a percent of national income are an interesting index.

side to maintain its "good life" its expectations of improving its condition in the future. Travel between various countries and even between continents reached unparalleled proportions after 1950; millions of Europeans and Americans and thousands of Russians and Japanese move annually around the globe for business and for pleasure.[19] Both trends have been made possible, of course, by a much higher standard of living in terms of the amounts of money spent by these people for purposes that are far beyond survival or the "bare necessities of life" and belong among the manifestations of the "good life." Migrations of laborers seeking better employment by moving across international boundaries have also affected tens of millions of people.

The economic trends of the early 1970s may interrupt the steady rise in all the curves reflecting international trade and travel statistics. A serious recession may set in for a while. Situations of scarcity and inequality may cause some return to more parochial or more nationalistic attitudes. A complete reversal of internationalizing trends is, however, unlikely. Elements of "worldwide" fraternity began to be recognized by scholars and some politicians in the 1960s through this growing economic and touristic (and therefore to some degree cultural) interdependence; these elements have planted seeds that are constantly fertilized by the flow of information daily streaming across borders by radio, television, publications, and exchanges of lecturers, students, and industrial manpower.

One may dispute the extent of the international goodwill and understanding that has been fostered in practice by the movement of people across frontiers. Tourists do not always return to their homeland full of admiration for the people of the lands they visit; their passage in those lands, while leaving some financial profits to the local people, does not often leave the best of memories behind. Large scale migrations of workers have at times caused local tensions, unpleasantness, and political moves to oust the foreigners. Nevertheless, on balance, the mixing of people, even for brief periods, gives the feeling of the possibility of living and working together. The flow of information about foreign countries thus acquires more meaning. A certain concept arises of belonging to the same vast interconnected system. New elements and ideas of universality take shape and gradually spread about.

The expanded and accelerated motion of people and goods from

[19] The number of French people travelling outside France every year in the late 1960s was estimated at 11 million (more than 20 percent of that nation); it was estimated at 8 million for the West Germans, and a similar figure for the United Kingdom.

country to country express both the need and the desire for some
degree of "internationalization" of modern ways of life. This trend
has also found a political and juridical expression in the various
international organizations that have proliferated in the last hundred years, beginning with such service institutions as the Universal
Postal Union (established in 1875), the International Red Cross,
and the International Labor Organization. More significant have
been the establishment and functioning in this century of the International Court of Justice (at The Hague), of the League of Nations, succeeded by the United Nations in 1945, and of the various
specialized agencies such as the World Health Organization, the
Food and Agriculture Organization, and the International Monetary Fund. The latter may be gradually becoming a powerful central clearing house for disputes and crises on the intergovernmental
level. Although deprived of coercive powers to enforce their rulings

14   The Communist Areas of the Old World in 1960. European countries are
indicated by their initials. The territory of the Soviet Union is heavily
shaded, outlining the area that has been behind the "iron curtain" since
1919.

strictly, these various institutions have greatly contributed to international public law, making it indeed a recognized body of legislation and laying down the house rules of an international community.

On a regional scale, groupings of states have advanced even further in pooling together the means of their exercise of sovereignty. The six participants of the European Economic Community since 1958 have offered the most striking and efficient instance of such developments in their formation of the Common Market. The regional grouping could be considered an attempt to work toward the merger of several adjacent states into a bigger one. In fact, each participant preserves a good deal of its sovereignty, and the ultimate outcome shapes a new type of political entity.

One set of boundaries, however, has acquired in recent times— first in 1919 and more definitely since 1945—a very special significance in the modern world: this is the line separating the communist countries from those of the democratic, liberal, and capitalist regimes. From 1919 to 1945 this line coincided with the boundaries of the Soviet Union. It was, on both sides, a highly guarded partition, difficult to cross. The Bolshevik Revolution of October 1917 had created a new situation in the world: a major power, especially in terms of size both in area and population, had adopted a political, social, and economic system utterly different from all those then existing in the world. The shock to the European political system was great—the greatest since the French Revolution. In the deliberations of the Paris Peace Conference of 1919, concluding World War I, relations with the new Russian communist regime were considered with much attention and many misgivings. The military leaders of the victorious Allied Powers proposed building along the European border of the U.S.S.R. a strong military barrier to prevent the expansion of communism, which at the time threatened to take over Austria and Hungary. A *cordon sanitaire* was to be set up around the communist area, as if to prevent the spread of a dangerous epidemic. In the discussions of the Council of Four, President Woodrow Wilson made a prophetic remark on March 27, 1919:

In my view, any attempt to check a revolutionary movement by means of deployed armies is merely trying to use a broom to sweep back a high tide. . . . The only way to act against Bolshevism is to eliminate its causes. This is a formidable task; what its exact causes are, we do not even know. In any case, one cause is that the peoples are uncertain as to their future frontiers, the governments they must obey, and, at the same time, are in desperate need of food, transport and opportunities for work. There is but one way to wipe out Bolshevism: determine the frontiers and open every door to commercial intercourse.[20]

The frontiers were first determined in the following period in a way that tried to strengthen the bordering states (Poland and Rumania especially) by giving them as much territory as was practicable.[21] After World War II, during which other political regimes proved more threatening to the western powers, the Soviet Union emerged as the second greatest world power; her armies occupied a large part of central Europe and some areas in the Far East. Communist-dominated regimes were established in a series of countries in the eastern half of Europe and linked by a tight military alliance to the U.S.S.R. A new frontier stretched across the continent of Europe, from the Arctic to the Adriatic, separating the communist and the western alliances and tightly closed by policies decided in Moscow. Winston Churchill described it as "the iron curtain" in 1946, and the expression became common in the political vocabulary. Although originally meant for Europe, the "iron curtain" description of the boundary around the communist countries applied also in Asia, especially after the Chinese Revolution of 1949 in which the communist regime led by Mao Tse-tung took over the whole of mainland China.

In the late 1950s, as the gradual "thaw" in the Soviet Union that followed the death of Stalin somewhat mellowed the totalitarian character of the communist regime, the iron curtain became less impenetrable, less sharp and rigid a partition in Europe. Still, the "Berlin Wall" and access to West Berlin remained a serious problem, a cause of recurrent tension and a constant reminder of the special and decisive role of that boundary in the modern world. It seemed that the new fluidity of people, goods, and information, characteristic of this epoch in the Western world, ebbed along this boundary line and barely connected through narrow sluices with another system of less fluidity, proper to the communist part of the world. The latter split soon into two major domains with the conflict between Moscow and Peking, between the doctrines and policies of the Russian and Chinese Communist parties. In the 1960s, however, more relations and more exchanges—diplomatic, commercial, and cultural—were gradually established across the iron and

[20] Paul Mantoux, *Paris Peace Conference 1919: Proceedings of the Council of Four,* trans. J. B. Whitton (Geneva, 1964) , p. 35; see especially pp. 30–36.

[21] This sort of policy was also advocated, though with some important nuances, by Sir Halford Mackinder in his book, *Democratic Ideals and Reality* (London, 1919) , which was much read and discussed again in America during World War II.

silk curtains. In 1971 the United States opened conversations with Communist China and authorized some travel and trade with that country.

The boundaries between communist and noncommunist countries remain on the whole more rigid and less permeable barriers than those within each of these two realms. They have, however, also been shifting in design and in significance. Intermediate situations have developed in Europe, such as those of Yugoslavia, for a brief period Czechoslovakia, and more recently Rumania. There are still two main groupings of powers, orbiting along different trajectories, although a numerous third category of independent states claims to be unaligned with either side either politically or economically. Still the iron curtain cuts across Europe in a very obvious way, and the main danger of general war seems to reside in the possibility of conflict between the powers on the two sides of it.

It is still characteristic of our time that this essential divide of the modern world separates two very different political and social doctrines. The basic opposition is in the domain of ideas, determining an opposition in cultural outlook and social structure. The iron and silk curtains are more linear than zonal because they are such sharp partitions; it may be said that since 1945 the *cordon sanitaire* is much more on the Soviet side of the curtain, endeavoring to prevent the spread into the communist realm of the ideas and products of the West. This boundary line looks from both sides of the fence rather like a frontier in the old Roman sense, separating civilizations that consider each other as barbarian. The exact delineation of the boundary was, however, agreed upon by both sides.

This examination of the modern role and evolution of international boundaries confirms the feeling of fluidity, of constant change, of search for a new international order. The decisive element in the evolution cannot be found in the boundaries, which are symptoms, effects determined by deeper causes. The "causes" are to be found by analysis in depth, and largely in the internal organization of the territory.

The Internal Structure and the Crossroads

The word *frontier* has been increasingly used in modern times in the sense of a broad change in the internal pattern of a nation's territory. In American history the frontier was a broad front of settlement advancing into essentially Indian-controlled parts of territory that was claimed to be already under American national sovereignty. In the 1890s Frederick Jackson Turner deplored the closing of the era of the frontier, which had swept the continent from the Atlantic to the Pacific and greatly contributed to the shaping of the American national character and to maintaining the social dynamism and the expanding economy of the country. But soon after 1910 he began to revise his views concerning the disappearance of this frontier: he saw it reborn, though with different characteristics, as the massing of population in the cities, accompanied by urban and industrial growth.[22] In recent years the expression "new frontier" has been widely and diversely used, serving as a motto for President John F. Kennedy's program.

This shift of the concept of the frontier from the wide open spaces to be settled to the dynamic crowding of metropolitan regions was more than a sign of a basic difference between the nineteenth and twentieth centuries in America. It was the recognition of the coming of a new order in the organization of the use of space as habitat. The passing of the long era during which the vast majority of men were toiling on the land to earn the means of existence by the sweat of the brow. The new, mechanized, automated age, in which information and knowledge were the main sources of prosperity, had to bring about a restructuring of the internal organization of the territory. This restructuring has been going on for at least half a century at an accelerating rate. Its results as yet are rather unsatisfactory, even in the richest and least crowded countries.

Into the concept of territory the new structure has injected a dilemma of considerable portent: the new complementarity between regions must rest on a spatial division of labor that increases rather than equalizes the contrasts between thickly and thinly populated regions over the whole extent of the territory. Urbanization, as we saw, and the specialization of certain nuclear regions in the geographical pattern of the national economy has caused in most modern states a concentration of population on small fractions of the territory. Cases abound today of independent nations that count 15 to 30 percent of their people in one or two areas totaling no more than 5 percent of their land area.[23] The migrations continue: more land is thinned of its population than is devoured by urban sprawl;

---

[22] F. J. Turner, *The Frontier in American History* (New York, 1920). The concept of the new frontier resulting from urbanization and industrialization is forcefully stated in chapters 9 ("The West and American Ideals") and 11 ("Social Forces in American History") both written after 1910.

[23] See above pp. 108–22 and also Jean Gottmann, "Grandeur et misères de l'urbanisation moderne" in *Urbanisme: Revue Française*, no. 88 (June 1965), 40–50.

only a few states, very small in area, do not conform to this general rule.

These trends sharpen the urban-rural conflict; they ought to have promoted the interdependence of regions whose production and ways of life are different but obviously complementary. The political process, however, has not allowed in its daily routine any harmony or agreement for a stable balance to be ironed out. The urban regions complain of being overcrowded, of not being given a fair share of the national budget, and of being poorly serviced by the countryside; the rural regions and small towns complain of being robbed of their people and resources by the overpowering attraction of the metropolitan areas. This is especially true in countries with a democratic, representative system of government. The increasing concentration of a majority of the population leaves large rural areas with a minority of voters. Some careful gerrymandering or special political party organization, sometimes both, have been employed to insure a strong voice for nonurban interests in the legislative assemblies. Practices of that kind, however, incense the urban populace and their leadership. The clash of interests that ensues hardly permits a well-planned, efficient restructuring of the land use, equipment, and servicing of the whole territory. Hence, the recent concern about legislative reapportionment and reform of local government in many of the Western nations.

This age-old conflict brings out a theoretical debate about the very essence of constitutional means of representation. The terms of the debate were well formulated in the opinions written by the United States Supreme Court in cases concerned with the reapportionment of electoral districts for the House of Representatives and state legislatures.[24] In 1958 the then Senator John F. Kennedy wrote: "The apportionment of representation in our Legislatures and (to a lesser extent) in Congress has been either deliberately rigged or shamefully ignored so as to deny the cities and the voters that full and proportionate voice in government to which they are entitled."[25] In the 1960s several decisions of the Supreme Court started a movement of reapportionment that is gradually correcting this situation.

Any given geographical distribution of political power is bound to try to perpetuate itself, although the geographical substratum that originally brought this distribution about may have been substantially modified. Besides an incumbent's understandable fear

[24] See Robert B. McKay, *Reapportionment: The Law and Politics of Equal Representation* (New York, 1965).
[25] *The New York Times Magazine*, 18 May 1958.

that he might not be reelected if his constituency were recast or, even worse, merged with another, there exists in all Western countries a deep-seated distrust of the political behavior of city dwellers, particularly as compared to the rural folks. England was not the only country to have had legislative assemblies dominated in the past by land owners.

In the American debate on reapportionment these important factors in the political attitudes toward urbanization came clearly to the fore. The Supreme Court decisions emphasised many times the need to redraw the electoral districts because of the migration from rural to urban areas. In 1962, in the case *Baker v. Carr,* Justice Felix Frankfurter said in his dissenting opinion that he thought the Court should allow legislative apportionment to rely substantially on "geography, economics, urban-rural conflict, and all the other non-legal factors which have throughout our history entered into political districting." The majority's subsequent decisions have not followed this recommendation. Basic principles of ethics were recalled when, in the famous decision of 15 June 1964 in the case of *Reynolds v. Sims,* Chief Justice Earl Warren stated that "legislators represent people, not trees or acres. Legislators are elected by voters, not farms or cities or economic interests. . . . The weight of a citizen's vote cannot be made to depend on where he lives."

In his dissenting opinion, on that memorable date, Justice Potter Stewart argued: "Legislators do not represent faceless numbers. They represent people . . . with identifiable needs and interests . . . which can often be related to the geographical districting." Discussing the apportionment for the Senate of New York State, Justice Stewart remarked that electing both assemblies of the legislature on the basis of equality ("one man, one vote"), as required by the majority of the Court, would put all parts of the state under the domination of "one megalopolis," a situation that seemed unethical to him.[26]

In the differences of opinion of these eminent jurists there are three disputed points that are significant to the evolution of the concept of territory as space and as organization. Firstly, the relationship between the political rights of an individual and the place of his residence; secondly, the role of territory in the political organization of the community; and thirdly, the balance of power between the metropolis and the rest of the political cell of which it is the nucleus.

The U.S. Supreme Court dealt, of course, with specific cases under

[26] *United States Reports,* Washington, D.C., Decisions and opinions, 15 June 1964.

the American laws. One may beware of the temptation to generalize too easily from this particular debate about American reapportionment. However, the opinions quoted refer to general principles of political and legal organization in a domain that is now being reviewed in most countries. Urbanization is a worldwide trend, and so is the greater mobility and affluence of the people, resulting in constant changes in distribution patterns, calling for reshuffling and even reform of local government. In this respect the three points arising from the American debate on reapportionment appear to be of very general interest, especially in the Western countries.

The first question, concerning the influence of the place of residence on the rights of the individual citizen, arises anywhere in the politically partitioned space. The partitioning determines a great deal in the individual's rights: it designates whether or not he is a citizen of a certain country, state, or city. The legal way in which the individual relates to the place determines whether he *belongs* in the community and, if he does, under which conditions and regulations. This was not always so in the past: in days of yore such matters could be raised only for free people and still would be tempered by the allegiance (for instance in the feudal system) a free man may have contracted toward another individual or group. Such arrangements of the past have survived in various parts of the modern world, despite its recent emphasis on nationalities, territorial sovereignty, and individual freedom. In many ways and in various countries an individual's allegiance to a religious sect, or a political party, or a special organization, affects his political (and in some cases even civil) rights. The general evolution of the laws have been nevertheless toward a doctrine extending freedom of individuals and equality of status. One of the major qualifications to the application of these principles, introducing the legal possibility of variation, was the recognition of sovereign jurisdictions within agreed territorial limits.

Within these limits, in every compartment, full equality appears to be repeatedly requested for the individuals who belong. This is certainly the meaning of the pronouncement that "the weight of a citizen's vote cannot be made to depend on where he lives," although the *nature* of that citizen's electoral and other political rights depends, of course, on the territorial organization of the place (country, city, county).

The second stage of the discussion now requires an examination of the role of territory in political organization. Generated by the people for their own purposes, politics, as a process and as a philosophy, may or may not take such environmental aspects as territory into account. Philosophy took it little into account, but the political process certainly did, and so did the legislator and the judge. Political districting was always and everywhere influenced by "geography, economics, urban-rural conflict," and other factors, as pointed out by Frankfurter; but practice in most fields, even those less disputed than politics, could make similar comments about "non-legal factors" influencing the framework of organization under the law. The constitutional laws in America had provided for electoral districts as equal in population as possible. Such numerical equality was obviously considered a guarantee that the interests of the majority would predominate over all the other factors and organized interests at play in the political arena.

Still, Justice Stewart's argument that legislators "represent people . . . with identifiable needs and interests" must be considered. Relating these needs and interests to a *stabilized* geographical districting assumes that the needs and interests will continue to be equally well served within a territory established on the basis of bygone patterns in a time of great change and fluidity. One may ask whether the old apportionment would not tend to reflect a set of old vested interests as opposed to the needs and interests of a modified community. The danger is that the territorial motive might be used either against a full expression of the will of the majority or against the adaptation of legislative machinery to the changes in the people's needs and interests that have developed since the previous apportionment in the region considered.

Territory thus appears to be a servicing structure established in the interests of the inhabiting community. It may be worthwhile to recall at this juncture the districting of local government and internal administration worked out by the French Revolution when it united the territory of the kingdom, erasing from the political map old provinces and other feudal fiefs and creating a new subdivision into *départements*. The constitutional committee of the *Assemblée Nationale* deliberated on the new division of the territory, which has remained to this day, with only small changes on the whole, as the basis of the administrative, political, economic, and electoral apportionment of France. The decisive report was submitted for the committee by Dupont de Nemours, in February 1790.[27] Although

---

[27] Assemblée Nationale, *Rapport sur le Décret général relatif aux départements du royaume, fait au nom du Comité de Constitution par Monsieur Dupont, député du Bailliage de Nemours* (Paris, le 13 [ou 15] février 1790). My translation from the French original as quoted in my *La politique des États et leur géographie*, pp. 126–27.

the demarcation of the *départements* followed, said the report, physical limits to the extent possible,

> a general principle has been adopted for these conventional lines, that the belfries will draw the parishes with the whole of their territory; that the chief-towns of the communities will carry along with themselves all the hamlets assessed on the same taxation rolls. . . . The maxim of Lycurgus "do not separate friends" has seemed to us to conform to your wisdom.

This interpretation of the general interest prevented the committee from following physical limits as much as it was intended at the start of the work.

> As to the rivers, which usually separate, except at the head of bridges and at ferries and other points of crossing, the civilian and religious establishments, your Committee endeavoured as much as it was possible to put the entire valley under the same administration so that a single authority could restrain the attempts occasionally made by riverside residents to increase their territory with alluvials and direct the power of the stream at their neighbours. There are rivers the banks of which must necessarily be protected, or rather there are none that would not require such care in more or less imperative manner; but it matters to the principles of societies which seek to preserve everyone's property that the works which are often indispensable along the banks of rivers, be conducted with utmost impartiality, and that none could be ordered on one side without taking into consideration their effect on the other side.

The great attention given in 1790 to river management as one of the bases of the country's districting takes on more meaning in the light of the modern concern with environmental control. Still, the main basis of the demarcation was the aim to allow "old friends" to live together within the same political subdivision. The human factor, as largely determined by the historical background, was predominant in shaping territorial patterns. Allowing for proper servicing of the community, and avoiding disruption of old linkages between a "center" and the surrounding area it served, were also essential considerations.

The fluidity of the mid-twentieth century challenged the division of France into *départements*. That urbanization was also a major cause was illustrated in the 1960s by the redistricting of the two central *départements* of the Paris region into seven new ones, and the creation of the status of *métropoles régionales* for a few selected cities, which were given new means to satisfy their needs by assuming wider functions of centrality.

A sweeping reform of local government, to come into force in the

1970s, was carefully prepared in Great Britain. The Report of the
Royal Commission on Local Government in England, usually referred to as the Maud Report, strongly set forth the need for a
smaller number of larger units to provide better for the present increases in numbers, density, and demands on the environment, especially in view of modern mobility and fluidity:

> . . . scientific discovery and industrial progress are reshaping the life
> and work of the people of England faster and more fundamentally than
> in any previous period of our history. The material on which local gov-
> ernment has to work, the situations that confront it, the patterns of settle-
> ment in town and country, have never stood still; but in recent years and
> in the years ahead they have altered and will alter in a quite new way.
> . . . In a period of great change, when huge unrepresentative organisa-
> tions seem to control the lives of individuals and restrict personal freedom,
> people might be tempted to give up as a bad job the effort to master these
> impersonal forces. . . . In this situation local self-government should be
> a crucial influence. It should represent the citizen and be the means
> whereby he brings his views to bear on those public problems that touch
> most nearly his personal and domestic life.[28]

The solution offered in the Maud Report has been hotly debated
as to local detail, and the ultimate districting once the reform is
applied may be at some variance from the map of the report's propo-
sals. But the general principles on which the solution was based are
worth recalling, as they are relevant to the discussions of similar
matters in other times and countries. The areas of local authority
appeared to need a definition enabling citizens "to have a sense of
common purpose." The commission concluded that the areas must
"be based upon the interdependence of town and country," and that
the inhabitants "must share a common interest in their environment." Two categories of services, the "personal" and the "environmental" were distinguished; the commission suggested that preferably both groups of services should be left in the competence of the
same authority, which "can relate its programmes for all services to
objectives for its area considered as a whole."[29]

The application of the principles was bound, however, to encoun-
ter various snags. Major difficulties were likely to arise immediately

---

[28] *The Report of the Royal Commission on Local Government in England,*
Chairman: The Rt. Hon. Lord Redcliffe-Maud (Cmnd. 4040) , 3 vols. (London,
1969) , and a short version of the Report, *Local Government Reform* (Cmnd.
4039) from which I quote (p. 2) .

[29] *Ibid.,* pp. 4–5.

in the cases of the large and dense conurbations; it must be pointed out that Greater London was kept outside the terms of reference of the Royal Commission, being a separate problem all by itself. This situation brings us back to consider the very important relationship of the role of the central metropolis to the territory. This question becomes all the more timely and weighty as concentration of population accelerates and as crucial economic activities concentrate in metropolitan or megalopolitan regions.

This trend has been observed, well documented, and analyzed in most advanced Western countries. Many governments have adopted policies of decentralization aiming at stemming or at least slowing down growth insofar as the largest national agglomerations are concerned. The less developed countries of Latin America and Africa have often bemoaned, even before the European countries began to do so, the rapid growth and increasing impact on the whole nation of one sector of territory in which population and economic activity was especially concentrated. Modern fluidity and urbanization have with few exceptions increased the trend of one-region dominance in the developing countries. A substantial difference between them and the countries of advanced economy resides in the fact that a very large proportion of the territories of these countries is empty and almost undeveloped, while the latter have in most cases developed almost all their lands rather well for the needs of the past (though there are notable exceptions such as the U.S.S.R. and Canada). The less developed countries feel they are missing more potential opportunities at home because of concentration, while the more developed feel they are adapting to modern needs but wish to avoid the inconveniences of crowding and to preserve some equality between their various regions. The two processes may be somewhat different, but they concur in deploring concentration and resenting the dominance of a central hub.

The dislike of the "domination by one megalopolis" as expressed for the state of New York in the opinion of Justice Potter Stewart reflects a traditional outlook of politics: the great, growing metropolis was distrusted, resented, and feared by the population outside it, in the country at large. The Bible, the ancient Greeks, and Mesopotamian tablets have spoken in unequivocal terms against Babylon and Nineveh. Plato deplored the rapid and large growth of Athens. Politicians have always been wary of large urban crowds. Sociologists have focused on the difficulties of urban neighborhoods. Finally, an ancient and constant conflict may be traced throughout history between the central government and the major metropolis in various countries.[30] These attitudes are too general and permanent not to be rooted in significant and constant causes. It may be useful to outline them.

Firstly, the great metropolis was the only substantial political power in a territory organized as one political unit that could challenge, even in the distant past, the organization of political power established over the countryside. In the political evolution of European nations since the Middle Ages, the city *bourgeoisie* after the fourteenth century and the urban working masses since the nineteenth have been the driving forces that took power away from the feudal barons and later the landed gentry whose strength was in the control of rural areas. This is only one facet of the matter, however, and a relatively recent one. The phenomenon we are dealing with is strikingly general: rapid urban growth and concentration are disliked even in the Soviet Union, where the historical heritage of feudalism and landed property has been efficiently swept away and could not influence present policy.

One must look at the specific structure of urban growth: it arises on crossroads, natural or manmade, and proceeds owing to its function of centrality, developing as a "hub." At a preliminary stage the city tries to set itself up as a crossroads for exchanges, either at a breaking point of transport, such as a seaport, a river confluence, or a portage between inland waterways, or at the contact of contiguous but different economic regions.[31] The beginnings are therefore linked not with the centrality in the original territory but rather with a peripheral position likely to attract the confluence of trade routes. Once such a crossroads is established, the men developing it work at weaving around it a web of outside relations, of which the city must remain the hub.

The development of the network and the maintenance of centrality imply several consequences that could hardly be to the taste of the inhabitants of the rest of the territory. Firstly, the city gathered at the crossroads people as diverse as possible, aiming at a cosmopolitan character and adding exotic components to its way of life. To the "good," more stabilized people of the surrounding country, suspicious of social fluidity, this appeared strange, alien, perhaps

[30] I have elaborated this point in my Special University Lectures in Architecture and Town Planning at University College, London, published as Jean Gottmann, "The Growing City as a Social and Political Process," in *Transactions of the Bartlett Society* (London, 1966–67), V, 11–46; partly reprinted in the *Southeastern Geographer*, IX, 2 (November 1969), 4–16.

[31] This remark was made by many geographers or historians who studied the origins of city locations, especially Jules Sion for Normandy, Paul Vidal de la Blache for France, and Chauncy Harris for the United States.

even sinful. Secondly, the business of commerce made the merchants in the city eager to obtain local products at the lowest possible prices while selling products from abroad at substantial profits. As producers and consumers, the people of the territory served by the city market resented such "exploitation." Thirdly, the interests of the city people extended far out along the lanes of their commercial network, and the city tried to commit the political unit or state to which it belonged to the economic and political support of such interests and the ensuing ventures. Fourthly, wealth and social status could be acquired in the central cities more rapidly, by means different and more diverse than in the countryside, where the social hierarchy was stable and more resistant to change.

These last two characteristics of the big urban center were particularly disturbing to the concern for political stability and an established social order; one way or another foreign participation led easily to foreign interference and adventure, while social fluidity increased not only the economic dynamism but also the political turmoil. These were the dangers of city growth, foreign trade, and maritime activity that Plato feared for an ideal city and sought to ward off in his *Laws*.

The tradition of condemnation of big cities is therefore old and respectable. Some conflict of interest must, of course, be allowed to exist between the hub living by and for a broad, long-range network of outside relations on the one hand and the surrounding population, suspicious of the aims and methods of the hub, on the other. A political unit of some size can hardly be built upon stability and homogeneity in the present interconnected, mobile, and changing world. Whatever organization of a political community is attempted, it will have to deal with internal structures of some variety, some oppositions and conflicts, requiring mutual tolerance and a desire for coexistence. No territory will know peace for any prolonged time unless its people agree to live together as a community, though stratified and diverse.

The modern proliferation of sovereign states has to a large extent granted the freedom of regional, almost local, self-government to many communities that sought for more independence. Reform of the internal structure, delegating more responsibility to local or regional authorities within defined territory, may help some of the larger powers to adapt better to the pressures and tensions resulting from modern fluidity. There are many different ways of reaching an internal balance. Virginia, for example, has had laws and customs different from those of the other states in its internal political partitioning. The rural-urban conflict, early recognized, has been dealt with by separating "independent cities" from the counties. In certain circumstances, however, a city may be permitted by the courts to annex part or whole of an adjacent county's territory. The procedure has not always worked to everybody's satisfaction, but it has allowed flexibility and evolution.[32]

The bigger the modern urban regions grow the more involved becomes their system of relationships with the territory to which they belong, especially on the national scale; in modern terms a very large city relates to a constantly broadening geographical area for the business that is conducted there, which allows it to subsist and grow. The large international hubs are linked not only by constant movement on the channels of transport and communications connecting them, but also by common purposes and interests. This grows increasingly disturbing to the outlying areas of the respective nations where the central hubs are accused of "extraterritorial" or "cosmopolitan" behavior.

"An International Social Function"

As the principle of the rights of nations prevailed in the evolution of constitutional and international laws, a symbiosis between a people and their territory developed in the form of the national state, on the modern European model. The partitioning of the world was coming in our time to be established on the recognition of the coexistence of many individualized sovereign states, each within its territory. In most international agencies every member state enjoyed a vote, irrespective of its size. Just as this order was reaching global proportions, after centuries of evolution, winds of change began blowing into the political arena, disturbing once more an apparently forthcoming stabilization. New currents in technology, economic demands, and political ideas have injected into the arena disquieting forces that expand accessibility, modify operating structures, and call for the revision of established concepts and principles. The resulting fluidity has turned the present situation into a rather chaotic state of affairs insofar as the meaning of territory and sovereignty is concerned.

[32] See Chester W. Bain, *Annexation in Virginia* (Charlottesville, Va., 1966), and *A Body Incorporate: The Evolution of City-County Separation in Virginia* (Charlottesville, Va., 1967); also John D. Eyre "City-County Territorial Competition: The Portsmouth, Virginia, Case," in *Southeastern Geographer*, IX, 2 (November 1969), 26–38.

Taking the long view to conform to the spirit of this analysis, one recognizes in the evolution of territory a new stage as momentous as that which occurred in the sixteenth century when the combined influences of the Renaissance, the Reformation, and the great discoveries brought territorial control and separation into the focus of politics. The contemporary stage results largely from a shift toward universal concerns of a decisive character. However, the new universality is very different from what underlay the Roman *imperium,* or at times the imperial power of caliphs and Chinese emperors. The new universality is truly global for the first time, encompassing the whole of mankind even statistically, and ultimately denying the existence of a category of outsiders or "barbarians"; but *the new order it seeks to promulgate is pluralistic by nature.* In this sense it integrates the juxtaposition of many varied territories, each of which supports a separate sovereign state. All these units are geographically and politically juxtaposed and interrelated. The present stage continues in a way the evolution that led to the emergence and proliferation of national states: a full territorial division has been achieved, most nations having been granted a territorial base with independence and self-government, and the fundamentals of security and equality appear to have been reached. On this foundation a new universal structure may come to rest.

In the present circumstances of military technology and of the circuits of the international exchange, the efficiency of sovereignty as a guarantee of security to the people has been much restricted. It nevertheless offers to the people the possibility of freely managing, within environing circumstances, their own affairs and their territory to the best of their ability. The territory assures the people a certain separateness, which is a condition necessary, although not sufficient, to their organizing for both security and opportunity.

While full physical security is today unattainable, short of a universal framework, a minimum opportunity is guaranteed by territory, as the latter is still the basis for any exercise of sovereignty. Sovereignty may have lost, at least for a time, its power of being *exclusive,* but it has acquired with international organization the value of a "union card" in all collective arrangements between states either on a regional or a global scale. Indeed the expression used by Judge Alvarez in his individual opinion in the *Corfu Channel* case (see above, pp. 6–7) must be appreciated: the sovereignty of national states is becoming "an international social function." The judge added the qualification "of a psychological character." As to territory, which evolves obviously on almost parallel terms with sovereignty, it is also now indeed "an international social function," but of a more material, concrete, and definite character, rather of a "psychosomatic nature" as already suggested here.

The territory provides a community with definite separateness, at least in terms of law and self-government; but it also provides the community with a capacity of complementarity with the outside, and ultimately with the world. This complementarity rests firstly on the material resources of the territory, which include location as well as the ability of the inhabitants (the total sum of labor, as Adam Smith would say, measured by productivity and other qualifications); and secondly, it relies on the privilege of sovereign states to participate with a vote in debates of international portent. Territory is the basis for some equality between states, whatever the variation in their size.

The territory continues to function as a portion of accessible space amidst modern fluidity. It has recently shown its capacity to expand in height with the advent of air space, laterally on the adjacent seas, in depth with the exploitation of the seabed and beneath. It has been limited in some respects, for instance in outer space. It keeps diversifying, subdividing, and reorganizing. But it has also acquired what could be called a new "social function," the right to share in the common wealth of the international community.

As the oceans are becoming an increasingly important source of a variety of valuable supplies and other advantages, one might expect that, in line with the five-hundred-year-old scramble for territory, the various states would extend their territorial claims over contiguous maritime spaces and the depths beyond them until all the formerly "high" seas are apportioned. Such developments would be in line with past history. What is new in the present situation is the talk about an international agency to supervise the use of the high seas and their resources; even more surprising are the attempts of all the landlocked states, from Afghanistan to Zambia, which see themselves being excluded from sharing in this new domain, to claim the right to participate in the benefits despite their locations. The principle of a right to share in wealth not yet appropriated merely because one exists as a separate political entity on one's own territory is fairly new; it illustrates the psychosomatic character of the territory as a new international social function; it also demonstrates that, in the present system, separateness generates complementarity.

Many various forms of complementarity are now developing on the international scale. Most of the well-recognized forms are intergovernmental in structure, and these kinds of agencies or organizations have multiplied in the last twenty-five years. The regional groupings are among the more tightly organized, though they all endeavor to preserve under some form the sovereignty and the territorial separateness of the participants. Some groupings, which cannot be called regional as they lack spatial continuity, cultivate older links due to a common cultural and political past, even though it may have been one of a "colonial" nature; the British Commonwealth of Nations and the French Community are the two most important examples of such groupings inherited from the dismantling of colonial empires.

More subtle but nonetheless significant are the linkages created between various countries by private or public organizations of a nongovernmental nature. In some cases, these are founded on cultural or religious links. In the economic field, national sovereignties are somewhat affected and nations interrelated by the networks woven in specialized domains by the great international corporations of modern business. Most of these are characteristically based in one territory and under the flag of one nation, but their diverse operations are so scattered and managed by so many agencies located in such dispersed fashion that to disentangle the puzzle and determine the "nationality" of each of the many components becomes a difficult task. Finally the growing interdependence of the great hubs of population and transactional activity scattered around the world adds to the involvement of each territory with others. Thus complementarity is reinforced in diverse ways. Despite the progress of certain aspects of technology, promising a possibility of more self-sufficiency for any territory containing a consuming market of large size, such trends will be counterbalanced for some time to come by the steady rise in the quantity and variety of per capita consumption.

The basic point about attempts at self-sufficiency within a limited territory is that people in general do not easily accept sacrifices for the sake of such isolation. For periods of crisis and as a method of regaining wider horizons later, policies of self-sufficiency may be locally and temporarily adopted. The constant and general purpose will rather remain that of unity, although the worldwide unity now envisaged is a pluralistic one, allowing for freedom and variety with diverse degrees and forms of complementarity. The concept of self-governing territory becomes the foundation of this pluralism.

The transition toward a new order of this kind has only recently begun. As one looks back it appears to be consistent with the mainstream of history; as one looks ahead one sees a long and eventful road to be travelled. Transitional periods of such portent easily last a few centuries and, despite the "acceleration of history," one cannot expect the partitions in the minds of people to shift quickly. Ideas of land as the basic resource for survival, of territory as the "sacred land of our ancestors," well worth the ultimate sacrifice to defend or to regain, remain alive for the great majority of mankind; they may still cause conflicts, wars, and suffering. Territorial irredentism is being cultivated by some nations. The view that acquisition of territory automatically insures a greater potential of resources and improves the prospects for a "good life" still survives and haunts many people. These dangerous conceptions belong to an old and respected tradition that helped in the past to bring some security to the territorial framework.

To allow some freedom in a political process that inevitably includes a struggle for power pursued with determination, the international as well as the national governmental agencies cannot strictly enforce stabilizing policies. The internal organization of territory will concern itself with the provision of minimum daily security. With the powerfully concentrated vested interests of great hubs, of huge corporations, and of a growing number of superpowers, the security of individual territories can only be assured on a collective basis and managed in the general interest. Plato's *Laws* may be recalled once more at this juncture, but with the exciting opportunity of our time, mankind has chosen to live dangerously. Perhaps the realization of the changes gradually wrought in the significance of territory may contribute to a safer operation of the spatial factor in politics.

Page-Barbour Lecture Series

The Page-Barbour Lecture Foundation was founded in 1907 by a gift from Mrs. Thomas Nelson Page (née Barbour) and the Honorable Thomas Nelson Page for the purpose of bringing to the University of Virginia each session a series of lectures by an eminent person in some field of scholarly endeavor. In a briefer form the materials in this volume were presented by Professor Jean Gottmann in March 1971 as the fifty-fourth series sponsored by the Foundation.

Index